AIMR Conference Proceedings
Equity Valuation in a Global Context

5–6 November 2002
Amsterdam

Richard Barker
Sophie Blanpain
Michael J. Brennan
Stefano F. Cavaglia
Pieter Dekker

Gerco Goote
Charles M.C. Lee
Patricia A. McConnell
Nicola Ralston, *moderator*
Barney H. Wilson

Association for Investment Management and Research

Dedicated to the Highest Standards of Ethics, Education, and
Professional Practice in Investment Management and Research.

> To obtain an *AIMR Product Catalog*, contact
> AIMR, 560 Ray C. Hunt Drive, Charlottesville, Virginia 22903, U.S.A.
> Phone 434-951-5499; Fax 434-951-5262; E-mail info@aimr.org
> or
> visit AIMR's Web site at www.aimr.org
> to view the AIMR publications list.

CFA®, Chartered Financial Analyst™, AIMR-PPS®, GIPS®, and Financial Analysts Journal® are just a few of the trademarks owned by the Association for Investment Management and Research®. To view a list of the Association for Investment Management and Research's trademarks and the Guide for Use of AIMR's Marks, please visit our Web site at www.aimr.org.

©2003, Association for Investment Management and Research

All rights reserved. No part of this publication may be reproduced, stored in a retrieval system, or transmitted, in any form or by any means, electronic, mechanical, photocopying, recording, or otherwise, without prior written permission of the copyright holder.

AIMR CONFERENCE PROCEEDINGS
(USPS 013-739 ISSN 1535-0207) 2003

Is published five times a year in March, April, twice in August, and September, by the Association for Investment Management and Research at 560 Ray C. Hunt Drive, Charlottesville, VA. **Periodical postage paid at Charlottesville, Virginia, and additional mailing offices.**

This publication is designed to provide accurate and authoritative information with regard to the subject matter covered. It is sold with the understanding that the publisher is not engaged in rendering legal, accounting, or other professional services. If legal advice or other expert assistance is required, the services of a competent professional should be sought.

Copies are mailed as a benefit of membership to CFA® charterholders. Subscriptions also are available at $100.00 USA. For one year. Address all circulation communications to AIMR Conference Proceedings, 560 Ray C. Hunt Drive, Charlottesville, Virginia 22903, USA; Phone 434-951-5499; Fax 434-951-5262. For change of address. Send mailing label and new address six weeks in advance.

Postmaster: Please send address changes to AIMR Conference Proceedings, Association for Investment Management and Research, P.O. Box 3668, Charlottesville, Virginia 22903.

ISBN 0-935015-90-6
Printed in the United States of America
April 10, 2003

Editorial Staff
Kathryn Dixon Jost, CFA
Editor

Roger S. Mitchell
Book Editor

Jaynee M. Dudley
Production Manager

Sophia E. Battaglia
Assistant Editor

Rebecca L. Bowman
Assistant Editor

Kelly T. Bruton/Lois A. Carrier
Composition and Production

Contents

Authors..	v
Overview: Equity Valuation in a Global Context........................... Nicola Ralston	1
Choosing the Right Valuation Approach................................... Charles M.C. Lee	4
Fusion Investing... Charles M.C. Lee	15
Evaluating Earnings Measures... Richard Barker	24
Quality of Earnings: Avoiding the Accounting Landmines................ Patricia A. McConnell	33
Risk and Return Properties of Global Equities.......................... Stefano F. Cavaglia Vadim Moroz	43
Adapting Fundamental Analysis for Cross-Border Valuation............. Sophie Blanpain	52
A Pragmatic Approach to Cross-Border Valuation...................... Gerco Goote	57
Reconciling the Numbers from Multiple GAAPs........................ Pieter Dekker	61
Valuing Hypergrowth/High-Uncertainty Companies—A Practical Approach............. Barney H. Wilson	70

Selected Publications

AIMR

Benchmarks and Attribution Analysis, 2001

Best Execution and Portfolio Performance, 2001

Closing the Gap between Financial Reporting and Reality, 2003

Core-Plus Bond Management, 2001

Developments in Quantitative Investment Models, 2001

Equity Portfolio Construction, 2002

Equity Research and Valuation Techniques, 2002

Evolution in Equity Markets: Focus on Asia, 2001

Fixed-Income Management: Credit, Covenants, and Core-Plus, 2003

Fixed-Income Management for the 21st Century, 2002

Hedge Fund Management, 2002

Investment Counseling for Private Clients III, 2001

Investment Counseling for Private Clients IV, 2002

Investment Firms: Trends and Issues, 2001

Organizational Challenges for Investment Firms, 2002

Research Foundation

Anomalies and Efficient Portfolio Formation, 2002
by S.P. Kothari and Jay Shanken

The Closed-End Fund Discount, 2002
by Elroy Dimson and Carolina Minio-Paluello

Common Determinants of Liquidity and Trading, 2001
by Tarun Chordia, Richard Roll, and Avanidhar Subrahmanyam

Country, Sector, and Company Factors in Global Equity Portfolios, 2001
by Peter J.B. Hopkins and C. Hayes Miller, CFA

International Financial Contagion: Theory and Evidence in Evolution, 2002
by Roberto Rigobon

Real Options and Investment Valuation, 2002
by Don M. Chance, CFA, and Pamela P. Peterson, CFA

Risk Management, Derivatives, and Financial Analysis under SFAS No. 133, 2001
by Gary L. Gastineau, Donald J. Smith, and Rebecca Todd, CFA

The Role of Monetary Policy in Investment Management, 2000
by Gerald R. Jensen, Robert R. Johnson, CFA, and Jeffrey M. Mercer

Term-Structure Models Using Binomial Trees, 2001
by Gerald W. Buetow, Jr., CFA, and James Sochacki

Authors

We would like to thank Nicola Ralston for serving as moderator at this conference and for writing the overview for this proceedings. We also wish to express our sincere gratitude to the authors listed below for their contributions to both the conference and this proceedings:

Richard Barker is senior lecturer in accounting at Cambridge University's Judge Institute of Management. His research focuses on professional investors' use of financial statement data. Dr. Barker is the author of *Determining Value: Valuation Models and Financial Statements*. In 1999, he received Cambridge's highest teaching award, the Pilkington Prize. Dr. Barker is currently on secondment from Cambridge University serving as research fellow at the International Accounting Standards Board, where he is working on a new international performance reporting standard.

Sophie Blanpain is head of equity research at Morley Fund Management, where she oversees global equity research. She is a graduate of the Institut d'Etudes Politiques de Paris.

Stefano F. Cavaglia is head of quantitative strategies at UBS Global Asset Management (Americas) Inc., where he is responsible for managing a long–short global equity market neutral fund and for developing quantitative models that cover the global equity universe. Previously, he worked as an economist at the Organization for Economic Cooperation and Development and taught finance at the City Business School in London. Dr. Cavaglia is on the editorial board of the *Journal of Portfolio Management* and is the author of many articles in academic and practitioner journals, including the *Journal of Banking and Finance* and the *Journal of International Money and Finance*. He holds an M.B.A. from the University of California at Berkeley and a Ph.D. from the University of Chicago.

Pieter Dekker is a senior manager in the Financial Reporting Group at Ernst & Young, where he specializes in financial reporting under International Accounting Standards. Previously, he focused on local and international audit engagements, initial public offerings, and the development of structured financial products. In 1996, Mr. Dekker was seconded to the European Commission's Internal Market Directorate General, where he was involved in the commission's work on financial reporting and the introduction of the euro. Mr. Dekker studied economics at the University of Amsterdam.

Gerco Goote is senior vice president and global coordinator of equity research at ABN AMRO Asset Management. He heads the global industries team, supervises the international integration of research in equity management, and oversees the global automobiles and components industry. Mr. Goote holds a master's degree in econometrics and industrial economics.

Charles M.C. Lee is Henrietta Johnson Louis Professor of Management, professor of accounting and finance, and director of the Parker Center for Investment Research at the Johnson Graduate School of Management at Cornell University. His research has been featured in the *Economist*, the *Wall Street Journal*, and the *New York Times*. Professor Lee is coeditor of the *Review of Accounting Studies* and associate editor of numerous other journals. He has received several best teacher awards and many research honors, including a 1999 Graham and Dodd Award of Excellence from the *Financial Analysts Journal*. Professor Lee holds a Ph.D from Cornell University.

Patricia A. McConnell is a senior managing director at Bear, Stearns & Company, Inc., where she serves as head of the accounting and taxation group in equity research. She is a certified public accountant and chair of AIMR's Global Financial Reporting Committee and past vice chair of the International Accounting Standards Board. Ms. McConnell has been named to the *Institutional Investor* All-America Research Team of financial analysts for the past 12 years. She holds an M.Ph. in economics and an M.B.A. from New York University.

Vadim Moroz is a quantitative strategist at UBS Global Asset Management (Americas) Inc., where he co-manages the quantitative long–short global equity strategy. Additionally, he is responsible for developing quantitative models covering the global equity and fixed-income universe. Previously, Dr. Moroz served as a research fellow at the Kaptiza Institute in Moscow, where he undertook fundamental research in experimental physics. He holds a B.Sc. and an M.Sc. from the Moscow Institute of Physics and Technology and a Ph.D. from Northwestern University.

Nicola Ralston is a nonexecutive director of two hedge funds and serves as a business advisor to CSTIM, a management consultancy. Previously, she served as head of investment management at

Schroders and was chairman of SIM (U.K.). Ms. Ralston is co-chair of the U.K. Society of Investment Professionals. She holds a degree in modern history from Somerville College at the University of Oxford.

Barney H. Wilson is chief investment officer at Lincoln Equity Management, LLC. Previously, he served as a vice president at Putnam Investment Management, where he covered semiconductor and Internet stocks. Additionally, Mr. Wilson covered technology stocks for American Century Investment Management. He holds a B.A. and a J.D. from the University of Virginia and an M.B.A from the University of California at Berkeley.

Overview: Equity Valuation in a Global Context

Nicola Ralston
Business Advisor
CSTIM Limited
London

This conference could hardly have come at a more appropriate time. A number of recent developments have caused investors to question the very core of their beliefs about how markets work. For example, much debate has occurred on the validity of the capital asset pricing model, the efficient market hypothesis, and the extent to which industry factors have become more important than country factors. Aside from these intellectual questions, investors have been buffeted by the collapse of the tech/Internet bubble and accounting-related scandals. The presentations in this proceedings attempt to shed light on these and other complex topics.

I have always been concerned about the gulf that often seems to exist between the world of academia and that of the investment practitioner. The danger is that each tends to regard the other with a degree of suspicion, concerned that the other operates in isolation, heedless of the added value that either greater academic rigour or the pressures of the marketplace might offer. Fortunately, the conference on which this proceedings is based brought together speakers from both worlds who were, almost without exception, extremely knowledgeable about each other's circumstances.

The speakers in this proceedings address some of the toughest issues in equity valuation, such as why a company's price moves so violently over short periods of time in the absence of a correspondingly large change in the company's underlying business performance, the dichotomy between the search for the absolute value of a firm and the dependence on relative valuation approaches, and the challenges inherent in deriving accurate valuations from accounting information. This proceedings provides excellent insight into current thinking on a wide range of issues pertinent to equity investors. The speakers meet the fundamental issues and potentially thorny issues head on, as well as discuss in depth the practical challenges faced by analysts and portfolio managers.

Valuation Models and Fusion Investing

Charles Lee presents two topics, valuation models and fusion investing; these topics are often viewed as distinct and unrelated, but he explains their conceptual similarities and how these two schools of thought are woven together to affect valuation. In his discussion of valuation models, Lee provides a detailed survey of the most common valuation approaches for equity and illustrates the impact of terminal value on the valuation process. He also discusses the main drivers and analytical implications of three common market multiples—price to book (P/B), price to earnings (P/E), and equity to sales (EV/S).

A great deal of subjectivity is associated with valuations derived from multiples; to remove much of this subjectivity, Lee recommends using valuation theory to select a subset of comparable companies from which a median multiple can be calculated. The drivers of each multiple are identified and strongly figure in the selection of the peer group of comparable firms. A "warranted multiple" is found for each company in the subset, as well as the targeted company. Companies are matched based on how close their warranted multiples are to the warranted multiple of the target company. Thus, through the judicious selection of comparable companies, the simplicity of the multiples methodology can be retained while removing a substantial amount of its subjectivity. This approach allows the integration of relative and direct valuation techniques and can be applied in cross-border analyses.

In his second presentation, Lee presents his case for "fusion investing," or taking advantage of the link between fundamental valuation and investor sentiment. Because the efficient market hypothesis fails to adequately explain all the fluctuations in stock prices and the persistence of systematic patterns in returns, Lee argues that analysts can develop more robust investment models by incorporating the findings of behavioral finance theory into their traditional models.

Basing his analysis largely on the work of Robert Shiller, Lee identifies three major implications arising from Shiller's model: First, as long as arbitrage involves a cost, then price will not typically equal value. Second, fundamental analysis is only one component of investing in stocks. Third, the time-series behavior of noise-trader demand matters. He also reviews more recent research, which indicates that prices are set in the dynamic interplay between noise traders and rational arbitrageurs, or fundamental value players, and that investor sentiment can cause prices to move away from their fundamental values. He concludes that both value and momentum indicators are variables that can be used to measure investor sentiment and that indicators of investment sentiment provide important clues about the dynamics between long-term reversals and short-term momentum.

Accounting Standards

Richard Barker's presentation transits two themes. First is a discussion on the use of alternative earnings measures in equity valuation. Second is an explanation of the new income statement under development by the International Accounting Standards Board (IASB) and forthcoming by 2005. Barker, whose role at the IASB involves drafting the proposal, outlines the goals of this project and addresses its possible effects on valuation.

Barker explains the various rationales behind devising a consistent definition of net income and stresses the importance of recognizing the subjective nature of earnings recognition and measurement. The income statement format that is likely to emerge from the IASB's efforts aims to maximize the predictive value of comprehensive income and its components by disaggregating total income and expenses based on their informational properties, such as operating versus financing and a category the IASB is calling "remeasurements." Barker believes that the new income statement will not only capture the critical components of earnings but also provide greater transparency for subjective measurements and increase the comparability of reported earnings.

As investors' concerns mount over the reliability of corporate accounting and reporting practices, Patricia McConnell argues that analysts should be especially cognizant of the potential landmines buried in and around three common corporate accounting challenges: pensions, employee stock options, and revenue recognition. In McConnell's view, the supporting accounting theory is simple, even though the assumptions and estimates incorporated in the calculations are not. Her dissection of the intricacies of pension cost components reveals that the widespread concern over the potentially huge liability that pension plans represent for companies may not be warranted. She predicts that the fair value method of expensing employee stock options will become mandatory in the United States (following the lead of the IASB) in the not too distant future. The result, she believes, will not be as negative as some companies' pro forma disclosures have so far suggested, mainly because history has shown that when companies have to account for a cost, they control it better. And the issue of revenue recognition, McConnell maintains, is particularly fraught with problems. Because most financial debacles have been caused by poor revenue recognition practices, she recommends that analysts carefully monitor the development of the Financial Accounting Standards Board's Emerging Issues Task Force Issue No. 00-21, which could potentially make sorting out the different quality levels of revenue recognition even more difficult than it is now.

Risk and Return Properties of Global Equities

Stefano Cavaglia and Vadim Moroz have found that a new paradigm exists for assessing the risk and return of global equity portfolios. Cavaglia provides a synopsis of their research into the way global businesses structure their operations in the 21st century and the subsequent ramifications for risk and return in global equities. The increasingly global structure of corporations has caused a shift from the predominance of country factors in valuation to the predominance of industry factors. Furthermore, cross-industry diversification is more effective than cross-country diversification in reducing portfolio risk, but the best strategy is diversifying across both country and industry.

Cavaglia presents the empirical evidence that supports conversion to this new paradigm and illustrates how a cross-industry, cross-country allocation framework can lead to better active global equity investment decisions. He demonstrates that a blend of forecast signals provides an effective way to predict both the short- and long-term return performance for local industries. These signals can be used to produce returns in excess of the world benchmark, even though conventional global risk models cannot explain this outperformance.

Cross-Border Valuation

Despite accounting incomparables and the complexities of global equity decision making, the prospects for pragmatic approaches to cross-border valuation are not hopeless. Although the first step in cross-border valuation is adjusting for differences in accounting standards among countries, Sophie Blanpain advocates that analysts concentrate on how a company's business practices can influence the way it operates. She provides several examples to emphasize the importance of this consideration in the valuation process.

Blanpain also highlights the areas in which ratio analysis fails to provide reliable comparative measures in cross-border valuation if accounting differences between countries are not taken into account. One of the most formidable problems, she notes, is that accounting P/Es can differ from real P/Es largely because P/E does not allow for economic-cycle adjustments. Nonetheless, she demonstrates that P/E can be a valuable tool under certain circumstances and that analysts should avoid at all costs getting bogged down in accounting minutiae at the expense of a fundamental understanding of a company's local business practices.

Gerco Goote also steers clear of a pure reliance on accounting numbers in his comparative analyses. He suggests that country- and industry-specific business practices play an even more critical role than accounting differences in cross-border valuation and offers the solution of sidestepping the accounting issues altogether by restating all items back to cash. Doing so allows the application of identical accounting schemes and the assumption of similar discount rates for similarly operated companies.

Goote further stresses the importance of considering qualitative factors (namely, the global industry and the company's business practices) before beginning a quantitative analysis. This global scenario approach can help pinpoint the kind of consistent value creation that creates long-term performance. An analyst's valuation ability will improve, he asserts, if the analyst thinks in terms of predicting a series of possible cash flow returns on investment (CFROI) instead of a single value from a discounted cash flow model.

Dealing with differences in accounting standards from country to country is a major challenge in cross-border valuation. Pieter Dekker maintains that, even though global harmonization efforts for accounting practices will continue to progress, differences are likely to persist for the foreseeable future and must be thoroughly examined before attempting cross-border analyses. He offers his expertise on the differences among International Accounting Standards, U.K. generally accepted accounting practices, U.S. generally accepted accounting principles, and various European GAAP frameworks that are responsible for the numerous incomparables complicating cross-border valuation.

Dekker outlines the major differences among accounting standards in seven areas: business combinations and goodwill, consolidation and special purpose entities, leasing, pension accounting, deferred taxation, share-based payments (employee stock options), and revenue recognition. He counsels that analysts who familiarize themselves with the various accounting practices followed in different countries around the world, as well as in particular industries, will have the best chances of avoiding suspect companies.

Valuing High-Uncertainty Companies

Barney Wilson has developed a model for valuing what he calls "hypergrowth/high-uncertainty" companies, which are not always adequately valued using the traditional valuation models. He explains why traditional valuation models often fail to accurately predict the prospects of hypergrowth/high-uncertainty companies and identifies three troublesome areas in using the traditional present value (or discounted cash flow [DCF]) methodology with these types of companies: the range for the critical variables, the discount rate, and the fade rate.

Furthermore, Wilson demonstrates the effectiveness of adjusting the DCF method through the use of scenario analysis, which focuses on a company's risk–reward potential rather than a point estimate of value. His adjusted DCF analysis results in a significant reduction in the model's sensitivity to the discount and fade rates, and eliminates the potential for disparate outcomes. A shorthand framework he has devised can be implemented on a daily basis, thereby facilitating the goal of determining the upside potential or downside risk involved in holding a particular stock rather than obtaining a single-point valuation.

Conclusion

As the components of the world economy become themselves more global and the acceptance of international diversification in asset management becomes more widespread, the task of cross-border valuation takes on great importance. Complicating this task, however, is a lack of harmony across accounting standards in the world today; the divergent local business practices of companies in the same industry; the complexities of accounting for pensions, employee stock options, and revenue recognition and their influence on reported earnings; and the implications of different valuation models and the information they provide. The presentations in this proceedings explain the issues, propose solutions, and highlight the areas in which analysts must be on their toes to avoid mistakes in valuation.

Choosing the Right Valuation Approach

Charles M.C. Lee
Henrietta J. Louis Professor of Accounting and Finance
Johnson Graduate School of Management
Cornell University
Ithaca, New York

> In picking a comparable company for use in multiple-based valuation, the choice depends on the multiple being used. Much better results can be obtained by using a warranted-multiple approach to select peer companies. One advantage of this approach is that it allows the integration of relative and direct valuation techniques.

This presentation has two objectives. First, I will explain how valuation models are related and provide a brief overview of the different valuation approaches for equity. In particular, I will focus on multiple-based and discounted cash flow (DCF) approaches and show how they are essentially two pieces of the same puzzle. Second, I will discuss a new valuation tool for equity that has emerged from academic research, focusing on recent research that uses a valuation-based approach to select comparable companies for multiple-based valuation.[1]

Equity Valuation in Perspective

Unlike rare art, stocks are presumed to have an intrinsic value. The intrinsic value of a Van Gogh painting is ill defined; basically, it is the amount that someone is willing to pay for it. But when equity analysts think of valuation, we think of intrinsic value. We have in mind a monetary sum that corresponds to the present value (PV) of expected future payoffs to shareholders. Equity valuation methods differ in technique, but they share the same objective—to estimate the PV of these payoffs to shareholders.

An obvious observation that follows directly from this definition is that equity valuation involves forecasting. Estimates of future cash flows, discount rates, and option values all involve forecasting what *could* happen to a company in the future. Some techniques, such as multiple-based approaches, may not appear to involve forecasting. In using these types of techniques, however, the analyst is taking a shortcut with the ultimate goal of forecasting a company's future prospects. In fact, it is probably useful for us to acknowledge from the outset that equity valuation is an imprecise science. It involves an educated guess, whereby analysts peer into an uncertain future and attempt to predict what a company might be worth.

No More New Economy. What about the "new economy"? We do not hear the term used much anymore. Only a few years ago, many were ready to discard traditional valuation models because the models failed to rationalize the successively larger market prices. The term "new economy" was coined to describe this new valuation environment. But exactly what has changed and what has not changed in the market and in valuation?

What has not changed is fundamental valuation theory; analysts are still trying to value a stream of uncertain future cash flows. What is different is the pace of change, which is extremely rapid. We live in a world in which the barriers to entry that have taken years to build can fall in just a few months. Forecasting is difficult in this type of environment, particularly for growth companies that will not see net positive cash flows until some distant point in the future. In this fast-paced world, the means by which

---

[1] Sanjeev Bhojraj and Charles M.C. Lee, "Who Is My Peer? A Valuation-Based Approach to the Selection of Comparable Firms," *Journal of Accounting Research* (May 2002):407–439.

Editor's note: This proceedings contains two presentations by Professor Lee. This presentation focuses on different valuation approaches. The second presentation, "Fusion Investing," discusses how behavioral finance relates to equity valuation. Although these two topics are often viewed as distinct, Professor Lee believes they share a number of similarities.

we estimate the key inputs to our valuation models (e.g., cash flows, cost of capital, and the value of intangible assets) are also changing.

Survey of Valuation Techniques. I will begin with a general overview. The arsenal of techniques available to analysts is divided into relative valuation methods and direct valuation methods. Relative valuation methods are those in which market multiples of "comparable" companies are used to value the target company. These include price to book (P/B), price to sales (P/S), price to earnings (P/E), and enterprise value to earnings before interest, taxes, depreciation, and amortization (EV/EBITDA). Direct valuation methods include a balance sheet approach, a contingency claims approach, and forecast-cash-flow approaches. The balance sheet approach values a company by valuing the individual assets and liabilities on the company's balance sheet; the contingency claims approach values a company as a basket of real options; and the forecast-cash-flow approaches value a company on the basis of the PV of the company's projected cash flows to shareholders. Each method has its advantages and disadvantages.

Of the three direct valuation methods, two are contextual in nature and are thus of less interest in general valuation. The balance sheet approach is often used in making lending decisions and in liquidation or distressed-company analysis. Its primary shortcoming is that it ignores the value of intangibles and assets in use (the fact that individual assets create value through synergy). In other words, most companies are worth more alive than dead. The contingency claims approach, although conceptually appealing, encompasses many practical problems related to parameter estimation. Because of these problems, I will focus my discussion on the remaining two approaches—forecast cash flows and market multiples.

■ *Forecast cash flows.* A forecast-cash-flow approach encompasses various derivatives of the dividend discount model (DDM), such as the DCF model, the Edwards-Bell-Ohlson (EBO) model, the economic value added (EVA) model, and the residual income model (RIM). All of these models are essentially the same; like different brands of camera, they work the same way. A photographer might prefer a Minolta to a Nikon, but all cameras incorporate the same variables—the amount of light entering the shutter is determined by the duration of the light exposure and the shutter speed. Likewise, all forecast-cash-flow models function according to the same principles.

These models also feature similar advantages and limitations. The main advantage is that they are conceptually sound and can be applied to most companies. The disadvantage is that they require explicit forecasting of future cash flows and discount rates. Some headway is being made on most of these limitations. For example, we now have a better understanding of the terminal-value problem—that most of the value comes in the later years of the forecast—and thus we are able to improve the estimation of terminal value. We are also making some progress in estimating the cost of capital. Finally, techniques are being developed to deal with the intangibles problem—the fact that new "knowledge-based" assets and other intangibles may have option values that are not reflected in short-term cash flow forecasts. But ultimately, the analyst's job in valuation is to forecast future earnings, cash flows, or dividends. The ability to make that educated guess gives life to a valuation model and is largely (and, perhaps, thankfully) still in the hands of human beings who can add value to this process.

■ *Terminal-value problem.* We can think of a company's value, or its expected cash flow, as having two separate components: The first is the PV of future cash flows *during* an explicit forecast period, and the second is the PV of future cash flows *beyond* the explicit forecast period. This second piece is called the company's terminal, or continuing, value.

The relative importance that the terminal value assumes in a company's total value is largely determined by the company's industry or production technology. For example, in an eight-year forecast period for a typical company in the tobacco industry, the continuing value typically represents 56 percent of the total value of the company; for sporting goods companies, the continuing value represents 81 percent; for companies specializing in skin care products, 100 percent.[2] For a typical high-technology company, continuing value typically represents 125 percent of total value, which means that the PV of the free cash flows for the first eight years of the company's life will be negative. In fact, all of the value of the company will derive from the expected cash flow beyond the first eight years. The terminal-value estimate truly is the tail that wags the dog when it comes to DCF valuations.

Figure 1 illustrates the way in which different valuation models deal with the terminal-value problem. On the left side of this diagram are the product and input markets of a company, and on the right side are the capital markets that provide the financing for a company. Inside the company are two types of assets—operating assets and financing assets. Net

---

[2]Based on data from Tom Copeland, Tim Koller, and Jack Murrin, *Valuation: Measuring and Managing the Value of Companies*, 2nd ed. (New York: John Wiley & Sons, 1996).

Figure 1. How the Three Types of Valuation Model Deal with the Terminal-Value Problem

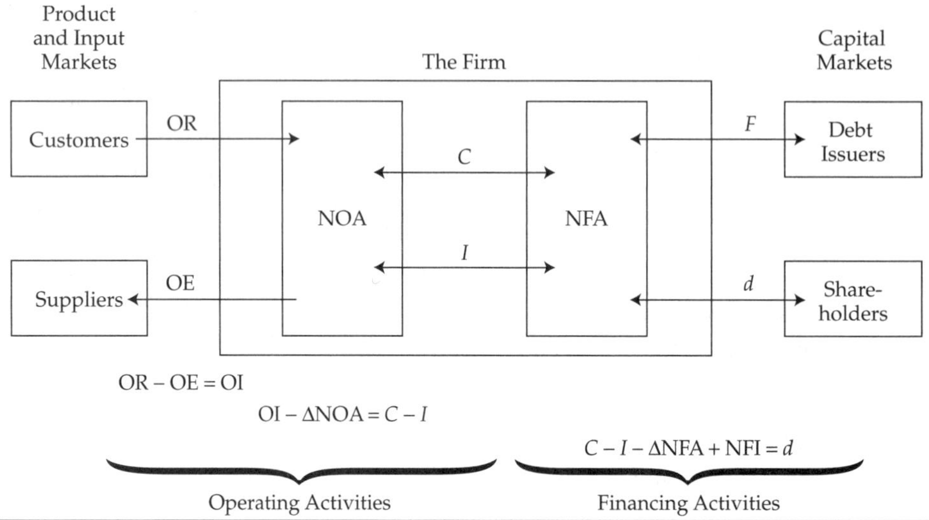

```
Product
and Input
Markets                              The Firm                      Capital
                                                                   Markets

Customers ──OR──►  ┌─────┐    C    ┌─────┐    F   ──►  Debt
                   │ NOA │ ◄──────►│ NFA │              Issuers
                   │     │    I    │     │
Suppliers ◄──OE──  └─────┘ ◄──────►└─────┘    d        Share-
                                                   ──► holders

OR – OE = OI
       OI – ΔNOA = C – I
                              C – I – ΔNFA + NFI = d
       ─────────────────────  ──────────────────────
        Operating Activities    Financing Activities
```

Source: Based on data from Stephen H. Penman, *Financial Statement Analysis and Security Valuation*, 1st ed. (New York: McGraw-Hill, 2001).

operating assets (NOA) are the wealth-creating engine of the company. Net financing assets (NFA) are assets and liabilities in which cash is "parked" until needed. The NOA of a company will increase as operating revenue (OR) increases and will decrease as NOA are used to pay operating expenses (OE).

A key measure shown on the diagram is free cash flow, or cash flow from operations minus cash flow from investments ($C - I$), which is the net cash flow between NOA and NFA. The cash flow to shareholders is represented by net dividends (d), or the dividends a company pays net of new equity financing, and is the net cash flow between a company and its shareholders. Cash flow to debtholders (F) is the net cash flow between a company and its debtholders. So, Figure 1 succinctly summarizes how cash moves in, within, and out of a company.

Figure 2 highlights the alternative cash flow measures on which each of the three models focuses. The traditional DDM focuses on net dividends. For example, the Gordon constant-dividend-growth model is based on forecasts of future dividends discounted back to arrive at a PV for the full set of dividend cash flows.[3] A complicating factor in implementing DDMs is that dividend payments are discretionary, and in fact, many companies do not pay dividends.

The key insight that gave birth to the DCF model is the observation that it is not dividends per se that matter but a company's *ability to pay* these dividends. By focusing on $C - I$, or free cash flow, the DCF model attempts to capture a company's ability to pay dividends, rather than the timing of the dividend payments themselves. The rationale is that it is irrelevant whether cash is paid out in dividends, as long as sufficient free cash flow exists to pay dividends if the company so desires.

The DDM and DCF are identical models. They simply focus on different cash flows, or more precisely, they focus on cash flows that are at different stages of the wealth-distribution process. The models merely attempt to estimate the amount of wealth that a company either *has* distributed or *can* distribute to its shareholders.

In the latest model developments, specifically the RIM, the focus has shifted to an earlier stage in the wealth-creation cycle. The focus is on OR and OE. The intuition is that these accounting-based performance measures can be used to estimate a company's wealth-creation capacity even before it actually generates free cash flow. The objective of an RIM is the same as that of a DDM and a DCF model: to measure the PV of future dividends. But the RIM focuses on wealth creation, whereas the other two models focus on wealth distribution.

Over the life of a company, the amount of wealth created must equal the amount of wealth distributed. But valuing a company by measuring its wealth distribution is a bit like trying to measure the activity

---

[3] For further information on the Gordon constant-dividend-growth model, see Myron J. Gordon, "The Savings, Investment and Valuation of a Corporation," *Review of Economics and Statistics* (February 1962):37–49.

Figure 2. How Different Valuation Models Focus on Different Cash Flow Measures

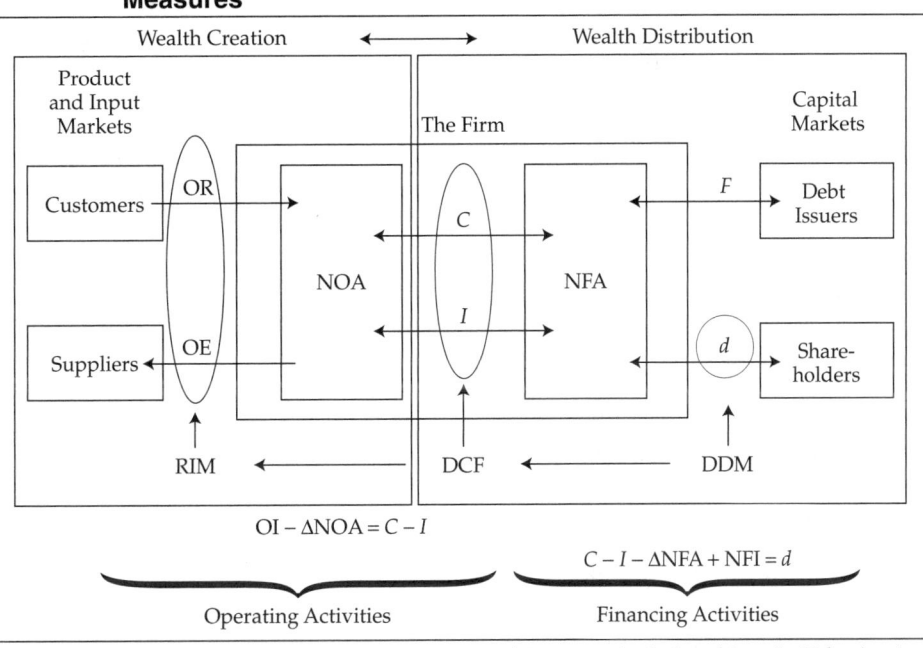

Source: Based on data from Stephen H. Penman, *Financial Statement Analysis and Security Valuation*, 1st ed. (New York: McGraw-Hill, 2001).

level of a factory by looking through its garbage bins. A sense of the factory's production level can be gained by counting the amount of garbage it is producing, but that is a rather indirect approach. By the same token, a company's dividends will give us a sense, but only a vague sense, of how much wealth it is creating. Over the life of the company, total dividends paid will equal total wealth created. But a more intelligent approach is to get a handle on wealth creation as it happens. Thus, we have witnessed a migration in the popularity of DCF models over time, from DDMs to DCF models to RIMs, as investors attempt to better capture the *source* of the wealth-creation process.

What is residual income (RI)? Simply stated, RI is the income earned over a given time period, minus the cost of the capital (in dollars) used to generate this income. The cost-of-capital measure is computed as the product of r (percentage cost of capital) and the asset base:

$$RI_{t+1} = Earnings_{t+1} - (r \times Capital_t).$$

RI is a single-period performance measure and is known by many "trade" names. For instance, Edwards and Bell (1963) and Ohlson (1992) both call it RI, Stern Stewart (1991) calls it EVA, McKinsey & Company (1995) calls it the economic profit model, and Palepu et al. (1997) call it abnormal earnings.

Regardless of your favorite handle for RI, the measure has a most attractive attribute—it boils down wealth creation to its three most elemental pieces: the earnings, capital base, and percentage cost of capital. If any one of these basic building blocks is missing, wealth creation cannot be measured. The key to an accurate company valuation is to consistently define each of the three building blocks as stated in the equation for RI: the asset base, $Capital_t$; the discount rate, r; and the expected cash flow earned on the capital, $Earnings_{t+i}$.

To transform a single-period RI measure into a multiperiod valuation tool, we need to estimate the RI for future periods and compute their discounted PV. The value of a company can then be defined as the PV of future wealth-creating activities (i.e., its future RI) plus the current capital base, such that

$$Company\ value_t = Capital_t + PV\ (Future\ residual\ income).$$

Alternative RIMs define the three key elements differently. A major distinction between the models is for whom the company is being valued—debtholders and shareholders or only shareholders. When we value the company from the perspective of both debtholders and equityholders, the capital base can be defined in one of three ways (NOA, net financial assets, and NOA with inflation and other adjustments), but the cost of capital is always the weighted-average cost of capital. When capital is defined as NOA, earnings is defined as earnings before interest (EBI) or net operating profit less associated taxes. Models that operate with these definitions include Stern Stewart's EVA and McKinsey's Economic Profit Model. Proprietary adjustments are typically made to the definition of earnings—Stern Stewart, for example, makes more than 100 adjustments in its EVA model.

When capital is defined as NFA, earnings is defined as free cash flow. The models using this set of definitions include the Alcar model (from Al Rappaport) and the traditional DCF model. When capital is defined as NOA adjusted for inflation, earnings is defined as EBI adjusted for inflation and other items. The Holt Value Associates' cash flow return on investment (or CFROI) model fits into this category. Again, the choice of model is a matter of preference; in reference to my earlier camera analogy, it is akin to choosing between a Nikon and a Minolta.

When the value of a company is of interest only to its shareholders, capital is defined as the reported book value of shareholders' equity under local GAAP. The cost of capital is the cost of equity, and earnings is defined as the earnings available to shareholders after debtholders have been paid. In other words, earnings is net income computed under the GAAP of the jurisdictional country. Models that follow this construction include Frankel and Lee (1998) and Penman et al. (1998).[4]

If company value is defined as the RI to shareholders, also known as EBO (Edwards and Bell [1961] and Ohlson [1995]),[5] the value of a company has to come either from the company's current capital base (book value) or from the PV of the RI created in the future. The following equation explains the methodology:

$$P^*_t = B_t + \sum_{i=1}^{\infty} \frac{E_t[(\text{ROE}_{t+i} - r_e)B_{t+i-1}]}{(1+r_e)^i},$$

where

P^*_t = the value of equity at time t,
B_t = book value at time t,

---
[4] Richard Frankel and Charles M.C. Lee, "Accounting Valuation, Market Expectation, and Cross-Sectional Stock Returns," *Journal of Accounting and Economics* (June 1998):283–319; Stephen H. Penman and Theodore Sougiannis, "A Comparison of Dividend, Cash Flow, and Earnings Approaches to Equity Valuation," *Contemporary Accounting Research* (Fall 1998):343–383.

[5] Edgar O. Edwards and Philip W. Bell, *The Theory and Measurement of Business Income* (Berkeley, CA: University of California Press, 1961); James A. Ohlson, "Earnings, Book Values, and Dividends in Security Valuation," *Contemporary Accounting Research* (Spring 1995):661–687.

r_e = cost of equity capital, and
ROE_t = return on book equity for period t.

Companies that are creating wealth will have an ROE higher than their cost of equity capital, r_e, so the term in the parentheses will be positive.

Market Multiples. I will now discuss the primary drivers and analytical implications of three common multiples—P/B, P/E, and enterprise value to sales (EV/S).

■ *P/B*. The EBO formula is useful because when both sides of the equation are divided by book value, we have the following:

$$\frac{P^*_t}{B_t} = 1 + \sum_{i=1}^{\infty} \frac{E_t[(\text{ROE}_{t+i} - r_e)B_{t+i-1}]}{(1+r_e)^i B_t}.$$

The left side of this equation becomes P/B, and the first term on the right side of the equation (book value) becomes 1. The result is an expression that helps explain the key economic drivers for the P/B ratio. (This equation, by the way, comes straight from substituting the clean-surplus relation into the DDM.)[6]

The first driver is the spread between a company's ROE (net income divided by shareholders' equity) minus the cost of equity capital. This term is commonly known as the "abnormal ROE." Think of abnormal ROE as an abnormal batting average. For example, in baseball, a typical third baseman might bat 0.250. But a player like Cal Ripkin might bat, say, 0.300; so, to mix the analogy, the abnormal ROE for Cal Ripkin would be 0.05. The second driver is growth in book value, which is future book value divided by today's book value. To stay with the baseball analogy, this element is equivalent to how often a player such as Cal Ripkin gets to bat.

The growth in book value is also a function of future ROE and net dividends. So, a company's P/B ratio is primarily a function of its expected future ROE. Companies that have expected ROEs higher than their cost of capital should have a P/B higher than 1. Companies that have expected ROEs that are lower than their cost of capital will have a negative numerator, causing their P/B to be lower than 1. In other words, wealth-destroying companies should trade at a P/B lower than 1.

■ *P/E*. Another common multiple is P/E. If earnings in the next period, E, is growing at the rate of g, then price equals earnings divided by the cost of capital, r, minus the growth rate of earnings, g:

---
[6] The clean-surplus relation is the assumption that changes in book value are completely captured by earnings or net dividends. In other words, $B_{t+1} = B_t + \text{NI}_{t+1} - \text{DIV}_{t+1}$.

$$P = \frac{E}{r-g}.$$

This expression is simple and intuitive, and it is easy to see that

$$\frac{P}{E} = \frac{1}{r-g}.$$

The P/E multiple is driven largely by the cost of capital and the growth rate of earnings. In a simple example, if the cost of capital is 12 percent and the growth rate is zero, the P/E will be 1/0.12, or 8.3. If the cost of capital is 12 percent and the growth rate is 7 percent, the P/E will be 1/0.05, or 20. Holding the cost of capital constant, the P/E ratio is primarily a function of g, the expected growth rate in earnings. High-P/E companies are those expected to grow their earnings quickly relative to today's earnings.

The P/B and P/E multiples do not necessarily provide identical signals. A high P/B indicates that the market is expecting a high ROE relative to a company's cost of capital. A high P/E indicates that the market is expecting high future earnings relative to current earnings. The two multiples are positively correlated, but their messages are not exactly the same. A high P/B says that a company operates in a profitable niche. A high P/E, however, indicates high growth potential for a company's earnings. A company can have a profitable niche but limited growth potential. Likewise, a company with strong growth potential can have limited profitability in the near term.

Table 1 is a matrix based on the P/B and P/E characteristics of six companies in the footwear industry. Companies with both high P/B and high P/E are "stars." Companies with a low P/B and low P/E can be referred to as "dogs." Companies with a high P/B and low P/E might best be called "falling stars." These are companies that have a profitable niche but not much earnings growth potential. Companies with a low P/B and high P/E are otherwise known as "recovering dogs." Recovering dogs have high expected earnings growth but low near-term ROE.

Table 1. Matrix of P/B and P/E Characteristics for Six Footwear Companies, as of 10 September 2001

P/E	P/B High	P/B Low
High	*Stars* Reebok International, Nike	*Recovering dogs* Wolverine World Wide
Low	*Falling stars* Timberland Company	*Dogs* Brown Shoe Company, Stride Rite Corporation

The P/Es and P/Bs of the six footwear companies that were used to construct the matrix in Table 1 are listed in **Table 2**. The median value for each multiple is used to define the quadrant classifications in the grid. Both Brown Shoe Company and Stride Rite Corporation are classified as dogs because their P/Es and P/Bs are below the median. Their multiples indicate that the market deems these two companies' ROE and earnings growth prospects to be lackluster. Wolverine World Wide is classified as a recovering dog based on its multiples—an extremely high P/E and a below-median P/B. At the time I compiled this data, Wolverine was only marginally profitable but had started to recover. Reebok International and Nike have high P/E and P/B ratios relative to the industry median and are classified as stars. Timberland Company is classified as a falling star. Although Timberland has products that enjoy a profitable niche, it lacks earnings growth potential. In summary, P/B and P/E both give us valuable information about how the market views a company, but the information they relate is not identical.

Table 2. P/E and P/B Data for Six Footwear Companies, as of 10 July 2001

Company	P/E	P/B
Brown Shoe Company	8.0	1.04
Stride Rite Corporation	14.1	1.31
Wolverine World Wide	57.6	1.91
Reebok International	20.1	2.76
Nike	19.4	3.23
Timberland Company	12.8	4.64
Industry median	16.7	2.33

■ *EV/S.* A third multiple that is useful in valuing a company is EV/S. EV/S is a function of a company's operating profit margin, controlling for growth and the cost of capital. Operating profit margins (PM) is the profit margins before interest, taxes, and nonrecurring items. For a stable company, enterprise value is the market value of a company's debt and equity:

$$EV = \frac{EBI}{r-g}.$$

EBI can also be thought of as sales, S, multiplied by PM because earnings is generated from top-line sales and the PM:

$$\frac{S \times PM}{r-g}.$$

As a result,

$$\frac{EV}{S} = \frac{PM}{r-g}.$$

Enterprise value, rather than price, is the appropriate numerator in this multiple because sales is a total enterprise concept. Sales belong to both debtholders and equityholders. The scale of a debt-free company's sales can be increased through additional borrowing. Thus, leveraged companies will look more attractive on a P/S basis than they should. The market generally recognizes this phenomenon. In fact, you will find that EV/S gives a much better fit in large-sample regressions than does P/S.

As the previous equation shows, a company's PM should be a key driver of EV/S. Companies with a high PM typically have a high P/S, but using P/S as a valuation multiple without controlling for the company's PM can be misleading. **Figure 3** illustrates the relationship between the P/S ratio and the PM for the 30 DJIA companies. As expected, companies with a high PM also have a high P/S or EV/S.

■ *Summary.* Multiple-based valuation is a peer-based relative valuation tool. In using a multiple, the analyst does not literally forecast the cash flows of the target company. Rather, the value of the target company is inferred from the market multiple ascribed to other peer companies. In other words, the analysis postulates that if the target company's performance is in line with the projected performance of the peer companies, the target company would be worth a certain value.

For example, the implicit question underlying use of a P/B ratio for valuation is this: If the target company can earn the same future ROE relative to its cost of capital as its peers, then what value should be assigned to the target company? When an analyst uses a P/E ratio, the implicit question is: If the target company can grow earnings at the same rate as peer companies, what would it be worth? And the same is true of EV/S: If a target company can achieve the same profit margin and the same future growth rate as its peers, what would it be worth? The fact that different multiples will yield different valuation results is not surprising because each ratio represents a different analysis.

Choosing a Better Comparable

Multiples are simple to apply as a valuation tool, but valuations derived from multiples can be subjective. That is not to say that a DCF model will not produce a subjective valuation, but the key to a good multiple-based approach is a judicious selection of peers. So, Bhojraj and I (2002) used valuation theory, or a valuation-based approach, to select the subset of comparable companies used to determine the median multiple for valuation purposes. Our approach is to identify the driver(s) of each multiple and systematically find the companies with the best fit based on those drivers and use them as the peer group. The next step is to find a "warranted multiple" for each

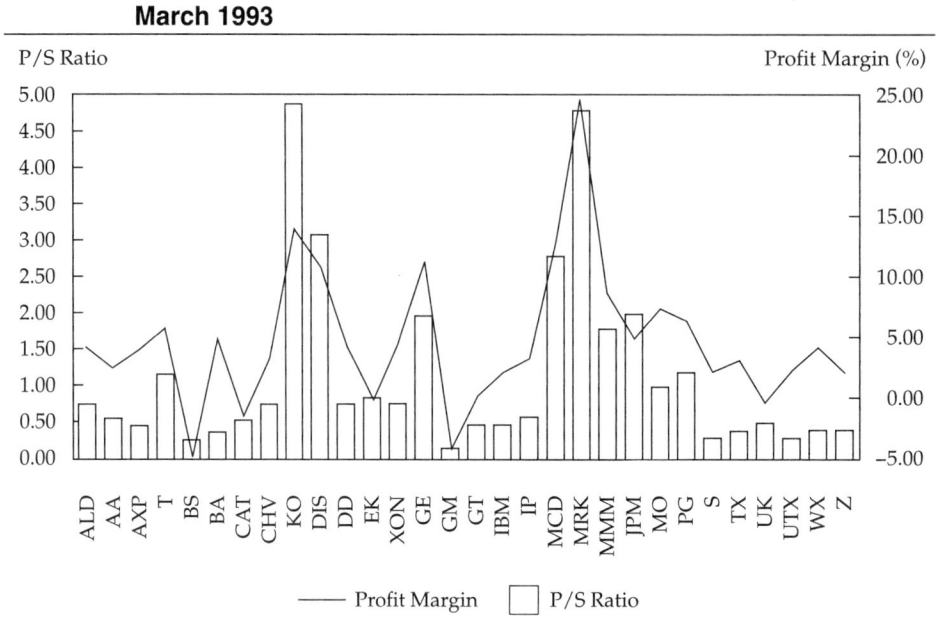

Figure 3. Relationship between P/S Ratio and PM for DJIA Companies, March 1993

Source: Based on data from Aswath Damodaran, *Damodaran on Valuation: Security Analysis for Investment and Corporate Finance* (New York: John Wiley & Sons, 1994).

company and then match companies on the basis of how close their warranted multiples are to the warranted multiple of the target company. Through judicious selection of comparable companies, the simplicity of the multiples method can be retained, but much of its subjectivity can be removed.

Two Key Issues. When multiples are used for valuation, two key issues must be decided. First, what multiple should be used? In other words, which fundamental accounting variable should be selected? Recent research shows that expected earnings on a two- or three-year forward-looking basis provides the best explanatory power for price and that sales has the worst explanatory power.[7] The median, or the harmonic mean, is the best measure for averaging multiples for many companies. The harmonic mean is simply the inverse of the average of the inverse. So, instead of averaging P/Es, average E/Ps and then invert that average.

Second, which comparables should be used? This choice is more difficult than the choice of multiple. In the past, research on the best choice of comparables has been based on expected growth similarities among companies and on an industry match (down to the three-digit SIC), but our research focuses on warranted multiples as the best method for choosing comparables.

Defining the Multiple. An important characteristic of a multiple is that the accounting variable used be consistently positive. For example, calculating a P/E for a company that reports a loss is problematic. As of 29 May 2000, of the 3,515 U.S. companies with more than $100 million in market capitalization and at least 12 months of data (excluding American Depositary Receipts), 776 were loss companies. Loss companies are companies with negative income before extraordinary items over the trailing 12 months. **Table 3** shows that to find a consistently positive result, it is necessary to move up the income statement. Of the 22 percent of loss companies, zero had a positive net income, 25 percent had positive earnings before interest and tax (EBIT), 40 percent had positive operating income, and 47 percent had positive EBITDA. Thus, more than half of the loss companies had negative earnings when defined as EBITDA, which would be meaningless if used to compute a valuation multiple. The only consistently positive number is sales. Book value is also generally positive; 94 percent of the loss companies had a positive book value. For this reason, in our research, Bhojraj and I used sales and book value as the accounting variable in our multiples.

Drivers behind the Multiples. P/B and EV/S are driven by similar factors: the cost of equity capital, r_e; short-term earnings growth rate, g; dividend payout ratio, k; PM; and ROE. The economic intuition underlying each driver is simple. The cost of equity capital reflects the riskiness of the company; PM and ROE measure the profitability of the company; g estimates the growth prospects for the company; and k indicates the level of reinvestment within the company. The loadings of the variables in the multiples, however, will differ. Based on our earlier discussion, EV/S should load more on PM, and P/B should load more on ROE.

Research Design. The first step that we took in our research was to estimate a model that would determine warranted EV/S (WEVS) values. We then ran a large-sample regression in which we let valuation theory tell us which company characteristics would help explain the differences in each EV/S ratio.[8] The market indicates which weight to place on each explanatory variable and estimates the WEVS for each company. The companies with WEVS closest

---

[7] Jing Liu, Doron Nissim, and Jacob Thomas, "Equity Valuation Using Multiples," Working Paper, UCLA and Columbia University, December 1999.

[8] The regression can be done across countries. We are undertaking research of this character now. See Sanjeev Bhojraj, Charles M.C. Lee, and David Tat-Chee Ng, "International Valuation Using Smart Multiples," Working Paper, Cornell University, 2003.

Table 3. Percent of Profit and Loss Companies with Positive Metrics, as of 29 May 2000

Type of Company	Number/ Percent	Net Income	EBIT	Operating Income	EBITDA	Gross Margin	Sales	FY1 Earnings	Book Value
Profit companies	2,739 (78%)	100%	100%	98%	100%	100%	100%	100%	99%
Loss companies	776 (22%)	0	25	40	47	87	100	34	94

FY = Fiscal year.

to that of the target company will be the company's peers. These companies have the best fit with the target company in terms of profitability, growth, and risk profiles.

To estimate WEVS, we used the following eight variables (most of which also work well in an international setting):

- *Industry EV/S (Indevs)*: The lagged median or the harmonic mean of EV/S for all companies in the same industry.
- *Industry P/B (Indpb)*: The lagged median P/B for all companies in the same industry.
- *Industry-adjusted profit margin (Adjpm)*: Company's PM less the industry PM. In other words, companies whose PMs are higher than that of the industry deserve a higher multiple, and those whose PMs are lower than that of the industry deserve a lower multiple.
- *Loss companies (Losspm)*: Adjpm multiplied by I, where $I = 1$ for loss companies and zero otherwise. This variable picks up the differential effect of losses, versus profits, on market multiples.
- *Industry growth adjustment (Adjgro)*: The company's forecast long-term growth less the industry's forecast long-term growth. Higher-growth companies should have higher multiples.
- *Leverage (Lev)*: Book leverage, or total debt to shareholders' equity. The higher a company is levered, the greater the inherent risk of the company.
- *Return on net operating assets (RNOA)*: This variable is intended to pick up other aspects of a company's profitability not captured by its PMs.
- *Research and development (R&D)*: Total R&D to sales; all else being equal, a company with high R&D expenditures will have high multiples. This pattern arises for two reasons: A higher degree of accounting conservatism found in companies with large amounts of R&D is being written off, and high R&D expenditures are indicative of potential growth options that are not valued in short-term earnings.

Table 4 gives the estimated coefficients, with accompanying probability values (*p*-values), for each of the eight variables. These results show that the eight variables explain a consistently high proportion of the variation in EV/S based on annual cross-sectional regressions from 1982 to 1998. The adjusted R^2 of about 72 indicates that 72 percent of the cross-sectional variation in EV/S can be picked up using these eight variables. The strongest explanatory variables are Indevs, Indpb, Adjpm, Losspm, Adjgro, and R&D. Notice also the reported *p*-values. These indicate the probability that each coefficient is significantly different from zero by chance alone.

The coefficients indicate how a particular company's EV/S ratio can be forecast. Specifically, the industry multiple can be adjusted for PM, expected growth, and level of R&D (because more profitable, higher-growth companies and companies with higher levels of R&D are worth more). The coefficients from this regression indicate how much weight to put on each of these company characteristics.

The preceding model estimation is used to identify peer companies by one of four methods. The first two methods are basically a simple industry and size match and the second two are based on WEVS:

- *IEVS*: The harmonic mean of actual EV/S for all companies with the same two-digit SIC code.
- *ISEVS*: The harmonic mean of actual EV/S for the four companies in the same industry with the closest market capitalization.
- *COMP*: The harmonic mean of actual EV/S for the four closest comparable companies based on their current WEVS.
- *ICOMP*: The harmonic mean of actual EV/S for the four closest comparable companies based on WEVS, in which the companies are constrained to the same industry.

Research Results. We find that the latter two methods produce much better EV/S forecasting results. The first two methods, simple industry mean and size-adjusted mean, explain only about 22–24 percent of current cross-sectional EV/S, with the adjusted R^2 ranging from 22.94 to 23.46. But as soon as other variables—PMs and earnings growth and so forth—are introduced, a much larger portion of EV/S can be explained. In fact, the latter two methods,

---

Table 4. Estimated Coefficients and Probability Values for Eight Variables, 1982–1998
(*p*-values in parentheses)

Intercept	Indevs	Indpb	Adjpm	Losspm	Adjgro	Lev	RNOA	R&D	R^2
0.1072	1.1277	0.0360	9.8043	–6.7162	0.0330	0.0184	–0.0052	0.0253	72.1
(0.007)	(0.00)	(0.031)	(0.00)	(0.00)	(0.00)	(0.235)	(0.00)	(0.00)	na

na = not applicable.

Note: Based on annual cross-sectional regressions.

COMP and ICOMP, explain approximately 60 percent of current-year EV/S.

One way to test the value of the estimation variables is their ability to forecast future EV/S or P/S. Industry- and size-matched peers explain only about 18 percent of two-year-forward EV/S. In contrast, COMP and ICOMP are able to explain about 50 percent of the EV/S of these companies, and three years ahead, from 45 to 50 percent. In short, a big improvement in forecasting ability is achievable by choosing the comparables used in multiple-based valuation.

This methodology for choosing peers also works for so-called new-economy stocks—biotechnology, technology, and telecommunication stocks. In that subset of companies, many are loss companies. Our approach of moving up the income statement and using sales as the multiple's denominator is particularly effective for this group of companies. In fact, the annual predictive power of our approach ranges from 58 to 84 percent. The coefficients used in the model estimation differ from those used for "old economy" stocks. R&D has a greater loading for this subset of companies, compared with the heavier loadings of the old-economy stocks on PMs and ROE. The heavier loading on R&D for tech companies makes sense, and the fit is good, even for the loss companies.

Summary

This presentation offers five lessons. First, in picking a comparable company for use in multiple-based valuation, the choice is dependent to a large extent on the choice of multiple. For example, the choice of a comparable for a valuation based on P/B should depend on ROE, and the comparable for a valuation based on P/S should depend on PM.

Second, much better results can be obtained if we use a warranted-multiple approach to select peer companies. In this approach, we start with the industry mean and adjust for PM, expected growth, and R&D. Because this approach is based on a DCF valuation model, we are able to find matching companies that have the closest overall match to the target company for valuation purposes.

Third, the warranted-multiple approach is applicable in cross-border situations. We are now taking the same approach to valuation using a pool of companies from the G–7 countries. Our preliminary findings suggest this technique works well in an international setting.

Fourth, an integration of relative and direct valuation techniques is possible when peers are chosen based on warranted multiples. The line between the two techniques has been blurred through the use of "smart" multiples. The "smart" comes from using DCF concepts to pick peers.

Fifth, RIMs and DCF models are similar in spirit. Their goal is the same, and with specific international applications, they allow for cross-border comparables.

Question and Answer Session

Charles M.C. Lee

Question: Does the formula work if the ROE declines with a higher book value?

Lee: Yes, the math works. But the key question is whether you can forecast ROE well. The task is more difficult for growth companies because the bulk of their free cash flow is generated further in the future.

Question: How long does the specific forecast period have to be to get the best result from the valuation model?

Lee: I can tell you what we do, but that doesn't mean our way is in any way optimal. I aim for a period of explicit forecasts that is long enough that I will not have to add another growth rate to the terminal value. Typically, a fixed period of about 10 years will do the job. If the explicit forecast period is long enough, I can simply assume a growth rate equal to the nominal GDP rate for the terminal value.

Question: Regarding the terminal-value problem, what is the discount rate used in calculating the PV of the cash flow during the explicit period and the PV of the cash flow beyond the explicit forecast period?

Lee: We use the same discount rate for both cash flow periods. We sometimes make an adjustment to growth for the cash flows in the terminal-value period that isn't made for cash flows in the explicit forecast period, so it may appear to be a different discount rate, but it is still $r - g$.

Question: The RIM requires the clean-surplus relation, which requires estimated dividends, so why not use the DDM? In other words, what is the advantage of the RIM versus the DDM?

Lee: That is a good question: If you're going to forecast dividends, why not simply use the DDM? In reality, a pure DDM is never used. Generally, in implementing a DDM, you still have to begin by forecasting earnings because dividends are paid from earnings. And in the terminal period of a DDM, you still have to assume 100 percent payout of earnings. The RIM is gaining in popularity over the DDM because a long-term forecast is easier to do when forecasting accounting numbers. The time-series behavior of accounting rates of return (such as ROA and ROE) is easier to predict than trying to come up with a long-term growth rate, g, in order to use a DDM.

Question: So, RI allows for better-quality forecasting?

Lee: That is generally true. Consider, for instance, a traditional DCF approach in which you do a detailed line-by-line forecast for 10 years. How do you know that you have made a sensible cash flow forecast 10 years from now? How do you know you've not made some inconsistent assumptions? The textbooks tell you to analyze the resulting financial ratios—asset turnover, PM, ROA, and ROE of the company 10 years from now. When you use a DCF model, you are still forecasting accounting numbers. You compute the cash flows and then check accounting ratios again 10 years later to see whether you've made reasonable assumptions.

In an RIM, you are explicitly forecasting the financial ratios. With consistent assumptions, the two methods should generate identical answers. But in selecting the right approach, consider focusing your forecast on the parameter for which you have the highest confidence. What do you want to forecast? Do you want to forecast earnings with a g rate or future accounting rates of return (ROA or ROE) with a fade rate? Forecast the number for which you have the tightest confidence band and let the valuation model convert that forecast into a company value estimate.

Fusion Investing

Charles M.C. Lee
Henrietta J. Louis Professor of Accounting and Finance
Johnson Graduate School of Management
Cornell University
Ithaca, New York

> Although fundamental valuation and behavioral finance are often viewed as divergent approaches, some research suggests important connections between the two. For example, indicators of investor sentiment may provide important clues about the transitional dynamics between long-term reversals and short-term momentum. Fusion investing is a relatively new approach that attempts to integrate traditional and behavioral paradigms to create more robust investment models.

In this presentation, I will lay the groundwork for a better understanding of the relationship between fundamental value and investor sentiment. The integration of these two elements of investing is called "fusion investing." I will discuss an integrative framework that can be used by value investors who also wish to think in behavioral terms. My thesis is that even a pure value investor needs to consider investor sentiment in formulating his or her strategy.

Efficient Market Hypothesis

In the traditional view of markets, the intrinsic value of a company is defined as the present value (PV) of its expected payoffs to shareholders. This PV is conditional on the information set available at time t, δ, such that

$$V_t = \sum_{i=1}^{\infty} \frac{E_t(D_{t+i} \mid \delta')}{(1+r)}.$$

Operationally, the efficient market hypothesis (EMH) is often interpreted as meaning that the price of a stock at time t equals the value at time t for all t, or $P_t = V_t$, $\forall t$. In other words, because the PV of future dividends cannot be known with certainty, the current price of the stock is the best proxy for V_t. For investors who subscribe to the EMH, the market is viewed as being extremely quick to reflect information relevant to future dividends.

At first, all the empirical evidence seemed to support the EMH. Researchers found that stock prices are hard to predict, and event studies indicated that prices adjust quickly to new information. In fact, in a 1978 article, Michael Jensen wrote, "I believe there is no proposition in economics which has more solid empirical evidence supporting it than the Efficient Market Hypothesis."[1]

But now, researchers are finding that even though returns are difficult to predict, prediction is not an impossible task; systematic patterns in returns can be observed. Researchers are also finding that prices adjust quickly but not in an unbiased manner. For example, a positive earnings surprise precedes a positive price drift. Furthermore, beta is not nearly as useful in explaining expected returns as theory suggests it should be. If beta is not already dead, it is surely comatose. Increasingly, the EMH—at least the proposition that stock prices reflect a company's fundamental value—appears too simplistic.[2]

The Behavioral Model

The behavioral finance literature has suggested an alternative to the traditional view of markets. In a relatively early study, Shiller (1984) introduced a simple model that illustrates the key dynamics in the

---

[1] Michael C. Jensen, "Some Anomalous Evidence regarding Market Efficiency," *Journal of Financial Economics* (June 1978):95–101.

[2] Charles M.C. Lee, "Market Efficiency and Accounting Research," *Journal of Accounting and Economics* (September 2001):233–253.

behavioral view of the world versus the traditional view.[3] In this model, only two types of trader exist: the informed trader (or smart money) and the noise trader. Smart money performs valuation analysis, such as discounted cash flow (DCF) computations, to calculate the PV of future dividends, whereas the demands of noise traders are motivated by whims, rather than serious valuation analysis. Noise traders have time-varying demands that are not based on an optimal forecast of expected returns for a stock.

In equilibrium, Shiller's model provides the following formula for price:

$$P_t = \sum_{k=0}^{\infty} \frac{E_t(D_{t+k}) + \phi E_t(Y_{t+k})}{(1 + \rho + \phi)^{k+1}},$$

where ρ is the expected real return such that there is no demand for shares by smart money and ϕ is the risk premium that would induce smart money to hold all the shares. This risk premium can be thought of as an arbitrage cost to eliminate market noise.

In short, the model says that price at time t is the PV of expected dividends discounted to infinity ("V"), plus an additional term. The first term, $E_t(D_{t+k})$, denotes fundamental value, the stream of expected future dividends. The second term, $E_t(Y_{t+k})$, represents the expected demand from noise traders, which is also known as investor sentiment. So, when noise traders are bullish, the second term will be positive and price will be higher. I think of ϕ as arbitrage costs. If arbitrage costs are zero, the second term drops out and price is only the PV of future dividends. In other words, if arbitrage costs are extremely low, $P = V$ and the EMH holds as a special case. If arbitrage costs are extremely high, the second term dominates and price is largely set by noise-trader demand.

Four implications are present when examining the market from the point of view of Shiller's model. First, price is not simply the PV of future dividends. Price is the weighted average of a stock's fundamental value and noise-trader demand. As long as arbitrage involves a cost, price will not typically equal value. Second, fundamental analysis (i.e., valuation and cash flow projection) is only one component of investing in stocks. In other words, the study of a company's fundamental value is only one part of the investment decision. Third, the other part of the investment decision (beyond fundamental value), particularly for smart money, is the demand from noise traders, which can have a substantial impact on the market. Thus, in addition to fundamentals, rational investors need to consider "fads" and "fashions."

John Maynard Keynes articulated this concept when he compared the market to a beauty contest.[4] The objective is to decide not only who you think has the prettiest face but also who you think everyone else will think has the prettiest face. In other words, the goal is to determine not only what you think the PV of future dividends will be but also what other investors think the PV of future dividends will be.

Fourth, the time-series behavior of noise-trader demand, or investor sentiment, matters. A value investor has to assume that Y_t is mean-reverting over a defined investment horizon. If Y_t is a random walk and today's Y_t is an unbiased forecast of tomorrow's Y_t, then price equals value plus a random walk, which, by definition, is not mean-reverting. If that is true, value could go in any direction—and value investors have a problem. The problem arises because, under these circumstances, the value investor cannot actually make money using fundamental value, particularly within a relatively short investment horizon. If the holding period is three days or three weeks, throw away your accounting book! If the holding period is three years, maybe fundamental value matters more. The success of value investing largely depends on how long it takes for the price to revert to the mean.

Investor sentiment can be measured two ways. One way is to focus on fundamental value by estimating the PV of a company's future cash flows, V, and comparing that value with the price of the company's stock. The difference can be thought of as a measure of investor sentiment. Another way to measure investor sentiment is to focus on noise-trader demand by identifying sentiment indicators that can help predict the direction of such demand.

Improving Valuation Models

First, consider the fundamental approach to valuation. In recent years, I have written a number of papers that have been aimed at improving the valuation model.[5] Taken together, the evidence appears to support the notion that a better estimation of V leads

---

[3] Robert J. Shiller, "Stock Prices and Social Dynamics," *The Brookings Papers on Economic Activity*, vol. 2 (1984):457–510.

[4] John M. Keynes, *The General Theory of Employment, Interest and Money* (New York: Harcourt, Brace & World, Inc., 1935), chapter 12.

[5] Richard Frankel and Charles M.C. Lee, "Accounting Valuation, Market Expectation, and Cross-Sectional Stock Returns," *Journal of Accounting and Economics* (June 1998):283–320; Charles M.C. Lee, James N. Myers, and Bhaskaran Swaminathan, "What Is the Intrinsic Value of the Dow?" *Journal of Finance* (October 1999):1693–1741; William R. Gebhardt, Charles M.C. Lee, and Bhaskaran Swaminathan, "Toward an Implied Cost of Capital," *Journal of Accounting Research* (June 2001):135–176; Sanjeev Bhojraj and Charles M.C. Lee, "Who Is My Peer? A Valuation-Based Approach to the Selection of Comparable Firms," *Journal of Accounting Research* (May 2002):407–439.

to better investment management performance. For example, in Frankel and Lee (1998), we used analyst earnings forecasts to compute a V estimate based on the residual income model and examined the usefulness of the resulting value-to-price (V/P) ratio in predicting future returns.

Table 1 is taken from that study. Our sample included all companies with analyst coverage between 1977 and 1991 (we stopped in 1991 to allow for three years of subsequent returns). To construct this table, we grouped companies into 25 portfolios as of 30 June of each year based on their V/P and book-to-market (B/M) ratios. The lowest-B/M companies are in Quintile 1 (Q1) and the highest-B/M companies are in Q5. Companies are also independently sorted based on V/P, with the low-V/P companies in Q1 and high-V/P companies in Q5. Table values represent the average buy-and-hold return for the companies in each portfolio over the next 36 months. The numbers in parentheses indicate the total number of observations (company years) in each cell.

In the far-right column and along the bottom row of Table 1 are the buy-and-hold returns for the three-year period following the formation of the portfolios. The bottom line of Table 1 reports the difference in return for extreme quintiles—that is, the return differential between the high-B/M (Q5) and low-B/M (Q1) portfolios, controlling for V/P. The far-right column in Table 1 shows the difference in return for the high-V/P (Q5) and low-V/P (Q1) portfolios, controlling for B/M.

For the B/M portfolios, the difference between Q5 and Q1 is minimal, meaning that B/M has little predictive ability for future returns over the following three years once we control for V/P. When B/M is controlled for, however, the V/P portfolios still have significant predictive ability for returns. In fact, the right-most column shows that the difference in return between high-V/P and low-V/P portfolios is between 15 and 47 percent for the following three years. This outcome indicates that a better valuation model can yield higher returns over the next three years. This is the good news.

The bad news is that, in the same study, we show that the price convergence to fundamental value is a long-term phenomenon. **Figure 1**, also based on the Frankel and Lee study, illustrates the cumulative monthly buy-and-hold return over 36 months for a long-minus-short B/M strategy and a long-minus-short V/P strategy. In other words, this graph plots the cumulative return for the Q5–Q1 strategy in the 36 months after portfolio formation.

Notice that in the first 12 months, both strategies return about 5 percent. After 24 months, the B/M strategy has earned a cumulative return of approximately 5 percent while the V/P strategy has earned a cumulative return of 17 percent. At the end of 36 months, the divergence in the return of the two strategies is quite striking. The V/P strategy has a cumulative return of about 35 percent, compared with a return of roughly 15 percent for the B/M strategy.

Table 1. Average 36-Month Buy-and-Hold Returns for B/M and V/P Portfolios, 1977–1991

B/M	Q1 (low V/P)	Q2	Q3	Q4	Q5 (high V/P)	All Companies	Q5–Q1 Difference
Q1	0.316	0.468	0.342	0.457	0.634	0.407	
	(998)	(592)	(296)	(264)	(269)	(2,419)	0.318**
Q2	0.366	0.461	0.489	0.415	0.516	0.450	
	(495)	(694)	(573)	(333)	(344)	(2,439)	0.150**
Q3	0.396	0.440	0.530	0.576	0.566	0.513	
	(295)	(515)	(660)	(565)	(453)	(2,488)	0.170*
Q4	0.350	0.422	0.484	0.589	0.630	0.535	
	(210)	(341)	(533)	(866)	(600)	(2,550)	0.280**
Q5	0.263	0.442	0.544	0.588	0.732	0.558	
	(386)	(328)	(433)	(510)	(824)	(2,481)	0.469**
All companies	0.331	0.450	0.491	0.549	0.637	0.493	
	(2,384)	(2,470)	(2,495)	(2,538)	(2,490)	(12,377)	—
Q5–Q1 difference	–0.053	0.026	0.202**	0.131	0.098	—	—

*Significant at 1 percent level.
**Significant at 10 percent level.

Source: Based on data from Richard Frankel and Charles M.C. Lee, "Accounting Valuation, Market Expectation, and Cross-Sectional Stock Returns," *Journal of Accounting and Economics* (June 1998):283–320.

Figure 1. Cumulative Monthly Buy-and-Hold Return for a Long-Minus-Short B/M Strategy and a Long-Minus-Short V/P Strategy

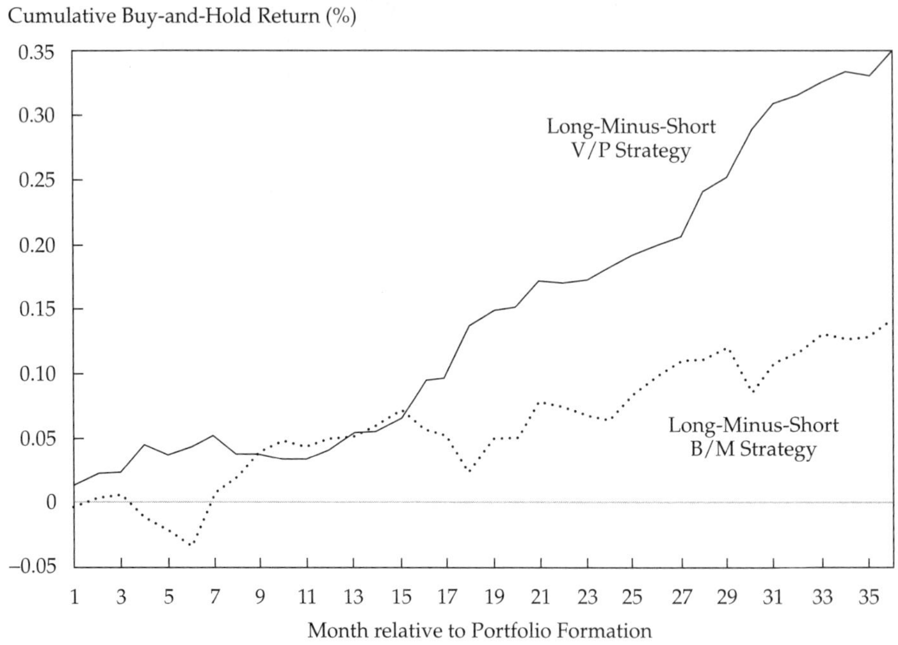

Note that the improvement in the valuation model yields higher returns only in the long run; after one year, the models produce approximately the same return. Clearly, the long-term nature of value convergence requires patience for an investor using a value-type strategy.

Another consideration regarding value plays is that they can be quite risky. Piotroski (2000) examined the returns of the top quintile of B/M companies—that is, the 20 percent of companies with the highest-B/M values, or value stocks.[6] **Table 2** presents the results of his study, which is based on data from 1976 to 1996. The market-adjusted mean return for this collection of high-B/M companies is 5.95 percent over a one-year period. Thus, value stocks as a group outperformed the market by about almost 6 percent a year.

But notice that the median of the return distribution is negative. In other words, the typical value company in this population underperformed the market by 6 percent. The reason value companies, as a group, outperformed the market is that the top 10 percent of companies have an average market-adjusted return of 71 percent. In fact, only about 44 percent of the value stocks actually outperformed the market (i.e., had positive market-adjusted returns in the one- or two-year period after portfolio formation).

Limitations of Value Investing. In short, value investing has its risks. It requires patience; abnormal returns are typically realized only over a two- to four-year investment horizon. Value plays can be

---

[6] Joseph D. Piotroski, "Value Investing: The Use of Historical Financial Statement Information to Separate Winners from Losers," *Journal of Accounting Research* (Supplement) (2000):1–41.

Table 2. Buy-and-Hold Returns for a High-B/M Strategy, 1976–1996

Return	Mean	10th Percentile	25th Percentile	Median	75th Percentile	90th Percentile	Percent Positive
One-year return							
Raw	0.2394	–0.3913	–0.1500	0.1053	0.4381	0.9017	0.6100
Market adjusted	0.0595	–0.5597	–0.3170	–0.0605	0.2550	0.7082	0.4369
Two-year return							
Raw	0.4788	–0.5172	–0.1786	0.2307	0.7500	1.5793	0.6457
Market adjusted	0.1271	–0.8715	–0.5174	–0.1112	0.3943	1.2054	0.4322

risky because the median value stock is no bargain; it underperforms. And buying value stocks typically means buying negative momentum because value-based signals and momentum-based signals are negatively correlated. Thus, picking value stocks usually entails running against a headwind, at least over the first 3–12 months, because value stocks tend to trend down over the short run. As a forecasting tool, value-based signals are more successful over longer holding periods.

Another limitation of value investing is that often an improvement in the valuation model contributes only marginally to return prediction. If a stock is extremely overvalued, it is overvalued based on practically every criterion—price to sales, price to book, price to earnings, and so on—and the same is true for an extremely undervalued stock. If the stock, however, is only marginally over- or undervalued, it will not revert back to fundamental value quickly.

What exactly is the problem with value investing? Fischer Black, in his 1986 presidential address to the American Finance Association, provided a key insight into this puzzle.[7] In this address, he discussed the role of noise in financial markets. In particular, he made the following observation:

> All estimates of value are noisy, so we can never know how far away price is from value. However, we might define an efficient market as one in which price is within a factor of 2 of value, i.e., the price is more than half of value and less than twice value. . . . By this definition, I think almost all markets are efficient almost all the time. "Almost all" means at least 90 percent.

In other words, Black claimed that we can consider the equity market to be efficient if price is within a factor of 2 of the PV of estimated future dividends. When I first read this statement, I thought Black must be exaggerating. Surely pricing errors could not be that big! But Black's contention is important because our priors regarding the size of pricing error and how quickly it will correct will determine the weight we choose to place on the value-based measures in our investment strategies.

Closed-End Fund Research. Research on closed-end funds (some of which I participated in) changed my mind about Black's assertion.[8] A closed-end fund is a publicly traded stock whose only asset consists of a portfolio composed of other publicly traded securities. Each Friday afternoon at the close of the market in the United States, every security in the closed-end fund is marked to market. Each Monday morning, the net asset value (NAV) of a share in the closed-end fund (calculated by dividing the total asset value of the fund's portfolio by the number of shares outstanding) is reported in the *Wall Street Journal*. The stock price of a closed-end fund is rarely equal to its NAV. This problem is known as the closed-end fund puzzle.

I think of closed-end funds as the one-cell amoebas of accounting. Scientists study the single-cell amoeba because it is a simple creature. Its transparent structure allows them to see everything that is happening in the organism. Similarly, the closed-end fund facilitates market research because it is not complicated by extraneous factors, such as deferred taxes and historical cost accounting. The closed-end fund is an extreme case of mark-to-market accounting, in which all assets are reported at their fair value on a weekly basis.

Closed-end fund stocks typically trade at a discount to their NAV [Discount = (Stock price − NAV)/NAV × 100]. Occasionally, however, they also trade at a premium. For U.S. funds, the discount routinely fluctuates between an upper bound of 5 to 10 percent and a lower bound of −30 to −40 percent. This condition gives rise to two questions: What accounts for the upper and lower bounds for the discount? And if arbitrage bounds can be this wide when valuation is transparent, how wide would they be for other stocks?

The answer to the first question is related to the availability of substitutes. The lower bound is explained by the fact that it is difficult to make money on a discounted fund unless the discount is quite wide. Because it is difficult to "open-end" these funds and the discounts themselves only mean-revert slowly over time, the typical retail investor can only expect a decent return when discounts reach 20 or 30 percent. The upper bound is more constrained than the lower bound because a new fund can be economically introduced to compete with an existing fund when the existing fund's premium reaches 8–10 percent (because total underwriting costs to start a new fund are roughly 8–10 percent of total asset value).

An examination of the second question—how wide arbitrage bounds are for nontransparent stocks—illuminates the point that Fischer Black made in 1986. Gemmill and Thomas (2002) examined U.K. data for closed-end funds and found that the level of the discount is a function of arbitrage costs.[9] In other words, on average, funds that are more

---

[7] Fischer Black, "Noise," *Journal of Finance* (July 1986):529–543.

[8] Charles M.C. Lee, Andrei Shleifer, and Richard Thaler, "Investor Sentiment and the Closed-End Fund Puzzle," *Journal of Finance* (March 1991):75–109. (*Editor's note*: For a review of the extant literature on the closed-end fund discount, see Elroy Dimson and Carolina Minio-Paluello, *The Closed-End Fund Discount* [Charlottesville, VA: Research Foundation of AIMR, 2002]; this monograph is available online at www.aimrpubs.org/rf/issues/v2003n2/toc.html.)

difficult to arbitrage tend to have higher discounts. Gemmill and Thomas also found that changes (weekly fluctuations) in the discount are a function of noise-trader sentiment, as proxied by retail-investor inflows to open-end funds in the same sector. When net flows are positive (negative), discounts narrow (widen) for funds in the same sector. The two results in this paper are important because they help us understand the interplay between value and momentum. Because prices generally vary within a fairly wide arbitrage band, value-based signals are not useful for predicting short-horizon valuations—except when the signals indicate extreme valuations. Effectively, prices are being set in the dynamic interplay between noise traders and rational arbitrageurs, or fundamental value players.

Measuring Investor Sentiment

Investor sentiment causes price to move away from fundamental value:

$$P_t = \sum_{k=0}^{\infty} \frac{E_t(D_{t+k}) + \phi E_t(Y_{t+k})}{(1 + \rho + \phi)^{k+1}},$$

where Y_{t+k} is investor sentiment. Investor sentiment is systematic and thus has to be correlated among noise traders. As a result, investor sentiment more closely resembles mass psychology than individual animal spirits. In other words, if I get an irresistible impulse to buy IBM and you get an irresistible impulse to sell IBM, our actions will have no effect on the price of IBM; our animal spirits do not constitute an impetus that moves multiple investors in the same direction, and thus our actions do not create the mass psychology that is investor sentiment.

Sentiment Signals. What gives rise to a common sentiment? One possibility is pseudo signals, signals that contain no real information but are persuasive in their own right. Another possibility is a suboptimal use of actual signals, an underreaction to such value-relevant information as earnings surprises and quality-of-earnings indicators.

■ *Pseudo signals*. Krispy Kreme Donuts (KKD), a U.S. donut maker, provides a good example of these types of signals. Through Internet chat room postings about the company, happy customers send pseudo signals to investors. For example, a visitor to a chat room remarked, "I can't understand how ANYTHING can taste that good. If this isn't the stuff classic American brand names are made of, nothing is. These things are addictive and they bring pleasure to the senses." People like these donuts, and they like the company because they like the donuts.

■ *Underreaction to actual signals*. KKD also serves as a good example for the suboptimal use of actual signals. As of 30 June 2001, KKD had strong positive momentum. Price was 12 times book and 6.5 times sales. Shorts in the stock were 41 percent of the total float, and the short ratio took four days of trading to cover. Particularly disturbing was that many insiders were selling and, over the 12-month period prior to the date of this analysis, the chairman of the board, Scott A. Livengood, had sold 95,000 shares that generated proceeds of $6,434,513—a bit more than it would have cost to send his kid to college! A DCF analysis, including residual income calculations, indicates KKD stock should be valued at $14 a share. If the market is assumed to be noisy, adding a fudge factor of 2 (in accordance with Black's premise) raises the price to $21 a share, still a long way below the 1 July 2001 price of more than $40 a share.

■ *Analysts' recommendations*. Another potential source of investor sentiment is the stock recommendations of sell-side analysts. I participated in a study titled "Analyzing the Analysts: When Do Stock Recommendations Add Value?," which compared the stock recommendations of analysts with the attributes that academics hold to be consistent with outperformance.[10] We found that analysts generally exhibit a strong bias in favor of growth stocks or glamour stocks with growth characteristics. Analysts get momentum right but everything else wrong. The stocks that receive the highest, most favorable analysts' recommendations tend to be the higher-P/E and higher-P/B stocks and tend to have higher trading volumes. They also tend to be stocks with higher income-inflating accruals, a characteristic that is negatively correlated with future returns.

If analysts are trying to predict positive returns, they should recommend positive momentum stocks. In fact, that is what they do; they give more favorable recommendations to positive momentum stocks. But the good news ends there. Turnover (total trading volume divided by shares outstanding) is negatively correlated with future return, so companies with higher turnover tend to underperform. Nevertheless, analysts more strongly recommend stocks with higher turnover, not lower turnover. Analysts should recommend higher-E/P stocks, but they more strongly recommend lower-E/P stocks. They should recommend higher-B/M stocks, but they more strongly

---

[9] Gordon Gemmill and Dylan C. Thomas, "Noise Trading, Costly Arbitrage, and Asset Prices: Evidence from Closed-End Funds," *Journal of Finance* (December 2002):2571–94.

[10] Narasimhan Jegadeesh, Joonghyuk Kim, Susan D. Krische, and Charles M.C. Lee, "Analyzing the Analysts: When Do Recommendations Add Value?" *Journal of Finance* (forthcoming 2003).

recommend lower-B/M stocks. They should recommend companies with lower long-term growth, but they recommend companies with higher long-term growth. Analysts should recommend companies with income-deflating accruals (i.e., companies with better quality of earnings); in fact, they recommend companies with income-inflating accruals.

We do not know why analysts' recommendations exhibit these biases. Perhaps, analysts are not really focusing on these variables. Perhaps, they are focusing instead on the incentives in their economic structure. Investment bankers like companies that exhibit high growth because they are the ones most likely to need their services, the ones most likely to need to come to the market for new cash. And the sales people and traders like companies with high volume and the greatest liquidity. Regardless of the incentives behind the recommendations, if the recommendations are taken at face value by investors, they will contribute to noise trading. Undoubtedly, analysts' recommendations contribute to prevailing investor sentiment.

Price Momentum and Trading Volume. Price momentum and trading volume are two variables that also help predict investor sentiment over short horizons. Swaminathan and I (2000) found that recent trading volume (shares traded scaled by shares outstanding) is a good indicator of investor sentiment about a stock.[11] High (low) volume stocks exhibit glamour (value) characteristics and earn lower (higher) subsequent returns. Integrating volume into the forecasting analysis greatly enhances the predictive power of the overall model.

The momentum life cycle hypothesis, illustrated in **Figure 2**, summarizes our findings about the impact of price momentum and trading volume on investor sentiment. We can think of companies as moving into and out of the glamour spotlight. There are times when they are out of favor with the market and times when they are in favor. The momentum literature calls the companies on the right of Figure 2 "losers" and the ones on the left "winners." Valuation provides a sense of whether a winner or loser is in the early stage or late stage of its momentum cycle. The typical momentum strategy supports buying all the winners and shorting all the losers.

Many market participants find momentum trading to be counterintuitive, or even anti-intellectual. A typical momentum investor buys the stocks that other investors bought over the past six months, and the higher the price moves, the more he or she likes the stock. Such an investment strategy does not seem to make sense. It is like a Ponzi scheme that is bound to collapse over time. Even though momentum strategies might seem profitable in backtests, investors shy away from them primarily because it is difficult to know when to exit such a strategy.

---

[11]Charles M.C. Lee and Bhaskaran Swaminathan, "Price Momentum and Trading Volume," *Journal of Finance* (October 2000):2017–70.

Figure 2. The Momentum Life Cycle Hypothesis

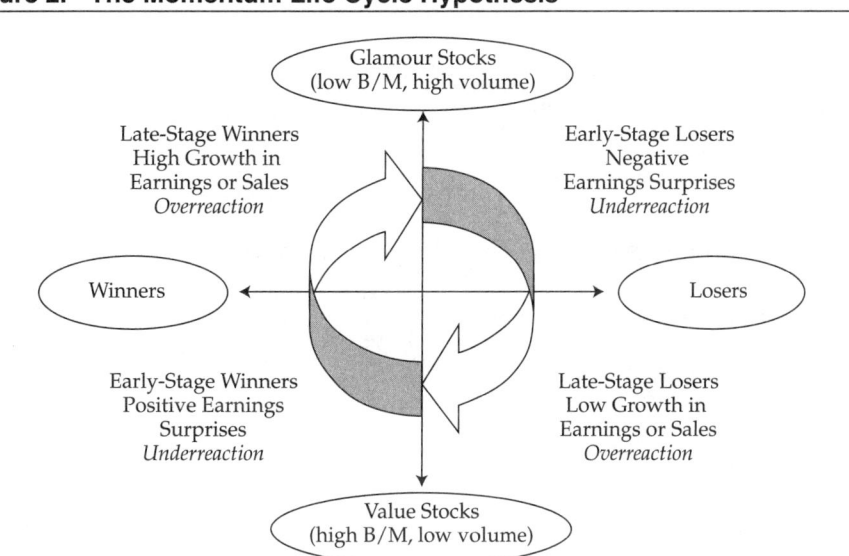

According to the momentum life cycle hypothesis, the game is to buy early-stage winners and sell early-stage losers. Notice that the strategy is asymmetric in terms of volume. The early-stage momentum strategy buys winners on low volume and shorts losers on high volume. The late-stage momentum strategy (which is far less profitable) buys high-volume winners and shorts low-volume losers.

The returns for the early- and late-stage price momentum strategies are quite different over a five-year horizon. **Table 3** (which is based on data spanning from 1965 to 1995) reports the raw returns for three price momentum strategies. The simple strategy is a Jegadeesh–Titman (1993) strategy in which the top decile of winners (R10) over the previous six months are bought and the bottom decile of losers (R1) over the previous six months are shorted.[12] This strategy produces an abnormal return of 12.49 percent in Year 1. But thereafter, in each year over the five-year horizon, the returns for the strategy dissipate.

The result for the late-stage strategy shows that reversing the direction of the trading volume when designing a momentum strategy can be costly. The return in Year 1 for the late-stage strategy—buying high-volume winners (R10V3) and shorting low-volume losers (R1V1)—is 6.8 percent, but nearly all of that return is lost in Year 2, followed by losses in Years 3, 4, and 5.

Conversely, an early-stage strategy—buying high-volume winners (R10V1) and shorting low-volume losers (R1V3)—generates a much more persistent return. The return to this strategy in Year 1 is 16.7 percent, followed by returns of 6.19 percent and 5.85 percent in Years 2 and 3. Remember that all three of these strategies involve buying winners and shorting losers. In this sense, they are all momentum strategies. But when the momentum strategy is conditioned on valuation and/or trading volume, the expected return can be quite different.

Figure 3 shows the Table 3 buy-and-hold returns adjusted for size. The difference in returns for each of the strategies is even stronger when the returns are industry adjusted. The "simple" line is the cumulative return for the simple long winner/short loser strategy. The "late" line is the cumulative return for the late-stage momentum strategy, and the "early" line is the cumulative return for the early-stage momentum strategy.

Panel A of **Figure 4** shows the returns for the winners (divided into two groups—high-volume winners and low-volume winners) for the sort year (Year 0), the four years prior to the sort year, and the five years following the sort year. Both high-volume

Figure 3. Size-Adjusted Buy-and-Hold Returns for Early- and Late-Stage Momentum Strategies, 1965–1995

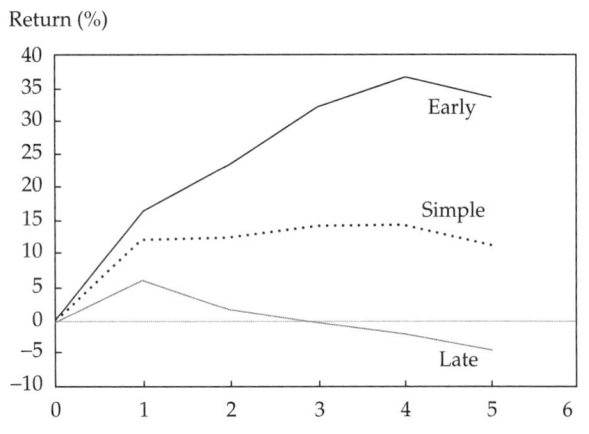

---
[12]Narasimhan Jegadeesh and Sheridan Titman, "Returns to Buying Winners and Selling Losers: Implications for Stock Market Efficiency," *Journal of Finance* (March 1993):65–91.

Table 3. Returns to Early- and Late-Stage Price Momentum Strategies, 1965–1995
(*t*-statistics in parentheses)

Strategy	Year 1	Year 2	Year 3	Year 4	Year 5
R10–R1 (simple)	12.49	–1.10	–0.32	–2.77	–2.96
	(5.04)	(–0.66)	(–0.15)	(–1.68)	(–2.46)
R10V3–R1V1 (late)	6.84	–5.35	–3.91	–6.33	–4.78
	(2.53)	(–2.17)	(–1.53)	(–3.54)	(–2.64)
R10V1–R1V3 (early)	16.70	6.19	5.85	1.53	–0.11
	(5.85)	(3.16)	(2.56)	(0.64)	(–0.06)
(R10V3–R1V1)–(R10–R1)	–5.65	–4.25	–3.59	–3.56	–1.81
	(–5.21)	(–3.00)	(–2.93)	(–3.14)	(–1.37)
(R10V1–R1V3)–(R10–R1)	4.21	7.29	6.17	4.29	2.85

Figure 4. Annual Return for Low- and High-Volume Winners and Losers, 1965–1995

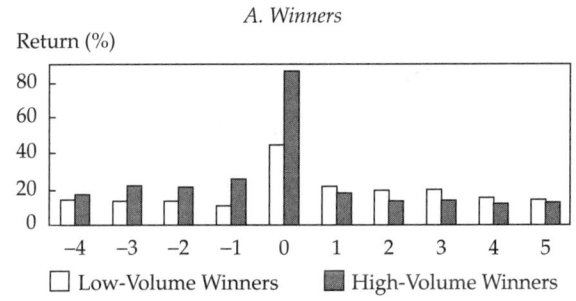
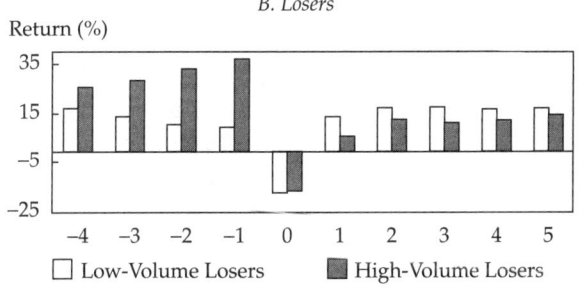

and low-volume winners have positive returns in Year 0. High-volume winners outperformed low-volume winners. The returns for high-volume winners were higher in the years before the sort year and lower in the years after the sort year. In other words, the high-volume winners can be thought of as late-stage winners that will not do as well in the future as they have in the past, and low-volume winners are essentially early-stage winners. Panel B of Figure 4 shows the same analysis for losers. Again, volume plays a role in the return prospects of the loser stocks. High-volume losers are early-stage momentum plays.

Referring back to Figure 2, the stocks in the top two quadrants (late-stage winners and early-stage losers) are glamour stocks and tend to attract the greatest number of analysts. The average number of analysts following the high-volume stocks is about 9. The average number of analysts following the low-volume stocks is about 3. Recall these numbers are conditioned on the fact that a stock is covered by at least one analyst. Otherwise, the stock would not be in this sample. As a company moves through its cycle, it loses analysts on the way down (as earnings and volume fall) and gains analysts on the way up (as earnings and volume rise). In short, analysts like momentum, or trend chasing.

■ *Momentum, volume, and valuation implications.* In summary, fusion investing takes the view that both mid-horizon-momentum and long-horizon-value effects are elements of a single process by which information is incorporated in price. Sentiment indicators, such as trading volume, help us to understand the transitional dynamics between long-term reversal and short-term momentum. In other words, sentiment indicators help us understand how a glamour stock essentially becomes a neglected stock.

When selecting stocks, it is necessary to think in terms of both value and momentum. For example, KKD has extremely positive momentum, extremely high volume, and extremely high valuation; it looks very expensive. In the fusion-investing framework, KKD is a late-stage winner. But how long can it remain a winner? No one knows. It depends on how the time-series behavior of noise-trader demand changes over time. Unless we can predict with some confidence when that positive momentum will turn, it is better to leave this stock alone, despite its lofty valuation multiples.

Summary

I have tried to argue that both value and momentum indicators are variables that can be used to measure investor sentiment. Momentum investors should pay attention to value because it can indicate when to sell, and an exit strategy is essential for momentum investors. Value investors should pay attention to momentum because it can indicate when to buy, and a crucial factor for value investors is knowing when to get into the market.

These are exciting times. A lot of the traditional paradigms, particularly the capital asset pricing model and the efficient market hypothesis, are being modified by behavioral theory. We are not discarding traditional models but working to create more robust models. A new brand of fusion research is emerging that integrates accounting and finance, fundamental and behavioral indicators, and noise traders and rational arbitrageurs.

Evaluating Earnings Measures

Richard Barker
Senior Lecturer in Accounting
Judge Institute of Management, Cambridge University
Cambridge, United Kingdom
Research Fellow
International Accounting Standards Board
London

> The inherent inconsistency and subjectivity in the measurement of earnings make a single, definitive measure of earnings virtually impossible. The International Accounting Standards Board is attempting to devise a new income statement and establish an accounting treatment that captures the critical facets of earnings and provides transparency for subjective measurements. The ultimate goal is a standard that can provide the uniformity necessary to make earnings measurements more useful and intelligible to equity analysts.

This presentation has two main themes. The first theme concerns the use of alternative earnings measures in equity valuation. The second theme is the new income statement forthcoming for International Accounting Standards (IAS) by 2005. In my role at the International Accounting Standards Board (IASB), I am responsible for the project of drafting this new income statement. The project is still at an early stage; an exposure draft is expected next year. My goal is to explain what we are doing, why we are doing it, and how a new income statement might affect valuation.

Note that this project goes beyond the IASB. We are working in liaison with the U.K. Accounting Standards Board and other major national accounting standards boards, including the Financial Accounting Standards Board (FASB) in the United States and standards boards in Germany, France, Japan, and elsewhere. This income statement project offers a clear opportunity for convergence. If income statements are not consistent from company to company and from country to country, then the appearance is that other reporting differences exist as well. So, a good starting point is the first page in the financial statements—the income statement.

Valuation Models

Two types of valuation model exist: multiples and cash flow models. (Charles M.C. Lee refers to them as relative valuation and direct valuation, but the principle is the same.)[1] These two categories are closely related because any given valuation model is simply a restatement of another valuation model. The simpler the model, the closer it is to being a multiple rather than a cash flow model. In effect, multiples are simplifications of more complex models. For example, a residual income, discounted cash flow, or dividend discount model can be reduced to a multiple by assuming constant growth rates. For analysts who would like to use a single performance metric in valuation (such as earnings per share), the assumption of a relationship between performance in the current reporting period and in all future periods is necessary, thereby enabling the use of a simple valuation multiple (such as the P/E ratio). With a more extensive valuation model, a simplifying assumption is not necessary because the relationships among the data are implicit in the forecasting.

Both types of model have similar information needs from income statement data—an understanding of the sustainability of earnings growth and

---

Editor's note: The views expressed in this presentation are those of Richard Barker and do not reflect the views of the International Accounting Standards Board.

[1] Please see Charles M.C. Lee's presentation, "Choosing the Right Valuation Approach," in this proceedings.

the identification of one-time events. The major difference is that multiples require a "magic" earnings number, such as operating earnings or pro forma earnings, whereas the free cash flow and the residual income model (RIM) do not. The free cash flow and the RIM are really just restatements of the same data. The residual income, or abnormal earnings, model, however, makes more explicit use of accounting data—earnings, book values, and so on—whereas the free cash flow model is less explicit.

Alternative Earnings Measures

In addition to the many standard models, many firms have their own alternative measures of earnings—operating earnings; pro forma earnings; normalized/standardized earnings; earnings before interest, taxes, depreciation, and amortization (EBITDA); net income; and comprehensive income. The first four measures are attempts to arrive at a normalized type of earnings measure that might be used in a multiple, whereas the latter two measures—net income and comprehensive income—are defined by accounting standards.

Net income is, in effect, common to income statements under both U.S. GAAP and International Accounting Standards. Comprehensive income is "one line below" net income and includes additional items that flow to a second performance statement (such as a statement of other comprehensive income) or directly to equity. Comprehensive income really *is* the bottom line and includes all income, expenses, gains, and losses (i.e., all changes in net assets other than those caused by transactions with owners). Comprehensive income includes all income and expenses defined under the International Accounting Standards Framework, whereas net income excludes certain items without having an obvious conceptual basis for doing so (items seem to be included and excluded in the calculation of net income for reasons of expediency). For example, gains and losses on certain financial instruments go below the line (i.e., they are not included in net income), whereas gains and losses from other financial instruments go above the line (i.e., they are included in net income), with no obvious explanation as to why the treatment differs. Gains on the revaluation of property, plant, and equipment (PPE) under international standards go below the line, whereas impairment losses on PPE go above the line. And the conceptual problems with net income are likely to grow because if items—such as goodwill impairment and actuarial gains and losses arising on pension obligations—are added to the income statement, they might be expected to go below the line. The tension caused by not having a consistent definition of net income is becoming a serious problem, one for which the IASB intends to find a solution.

The net income figure itself is arguably not very useful to financial analysts. The proliferation of operating earnings-type numbers would not have occurred if net income was a good measure of a company's performance. The multiplicity of earnings numbers is a problem. The following quote appeared in the *Wall Street Journal*: "The 'E' used to refer to earnings under GAAP . . . [but now it refers to] 'operating earnings' . . . (i.e., whatever a company wants it to mean)."[2] The article demonstrates the magnitude of the problem by comparing the P/E ratio for the S&P 500 Index using the operating earnings number and the net income number (note that the data are not current). Based on net income as reported under U.S. GAAP, the P/E was 36.7, in which case the market seemed quite expensive. Based on operating earnings as reported by Thomson Financial/First Call, however, the P/E was 22.2, in which case the market did not look expensive. The difference between the two numbers is huge and is approximately equal to the long-run average P/E ratio. Although the example is not based on current data, the same problem persists today.

A specific company example of a wide differential between alternative income measures is Cisco Systems. In 2001, Cisco reported pro forma income of $3.09 billion, compared with $3.91 billion in 2000. In effect, Cisco was promoting pro forma net income as the headline number for its annual performance. Further down the page, however, Cisco reported an actual net loss in 2001 of $1.01 billion, which is a difference of about $4 billion relative to the pro forma. The absolute magnitude of the difference is unusual, but relative to the size of the company, it is not an abnormally large difference.

Now, consider the nature of some of Cisco's adjustments. The company had restructuring costs of $1.2 billion (severance costs of $400 million, consolidation costs of $500 million, and goodwill impairment of $300 million). In addition, the company had an excess inventory charge of $900 million and goodwill amortization and "other" charges amounting to $1.2 billion.

From a standard-setting point of view and in terms of presenting this information consistently and comparably for different entities, the issue is how to rationalize reporting some components of company performance differently from others and reporting some components below the line and some above the

---

[2]*Wall Street Journal*, "What's the PE Ratio? Well, It Depends on What Is Meant by Earnings" (21 August 2001).

line. Various rationales are possible—making a split between operating and nonoperating income, between recurring and one-time costs, between core and noncore earnings, and between items within management's control and items outside management's control.

Much overlap exists between these different conceptual approaches. Often, the distinction is drawn based on the frequency with which an entity engages in a certain activity. On the one hand, the sale of a retail company's inventory is an ongoing activity. But if a retailer sells one of its stores, which is not a retailer's usual sort of business, the gain on the sale is reported as one-time, nonoperating, noncore income. Although selling inventory and selling a store both amount to selling an asset for a gain or a loss, making a core/noncore distinction is reasonable. On the other hand, if the retail company has a real estate portfolio and manages this portfolio, rather than simply engaging in an occasional sale of real estate, such fairly frequent buying and selling of real estate seems to constitute an operating activity. And certainly, for a real estate company, the buying and selling of real estate is the core activity. The result is a classification based on a sliding scale of the type of business and the frequency of a given activity. The problem with this sliding scale is that any attempt by standard setters, analysts, or companies to draw a definitive line in the sand as to what qualifies for nonoperating and operating income is bound to be vulnerable to abuse, subjectivity, and inconsistency.

Consider another specific company illustration. For 2001, Unilever had total operating profit of €5.258 billion and total operating profit before exceptional items and amortization of €7.269 billion. The difference of roughly €2 billion equaled the company's exceptional items and amortization, which included restructuring costs of €1.5 billion, disposal gains of €900 million, and amortization of goodwill and intangibles equal to €1.4 billion.

To say the restructuring costs, disposal gains, and amortization of goodwill are one-time, nonoperating, noncore income is reasonable. But when a major criterion for classifying an item as exceptional is the item's size, the subjective nature of that judgment encourages inconsistencies in treatment and reporting. For example, at what point did the inventory impairment for Cisco become an unusual item, as opposed to a normal inventory write-off? If Cisco wants to highlight its inventory impairment, perhaps it ought to do so within the cost-of-sales line. It is arguably unhelpful to have cost of sales in one place and unusual inventory impairments further down the income statement. Both inventory value changes could be shown in the same place. Similarly, the separate display of restructuring charges can be difficult to defend, and there is scope for misinformation.

Not only is defining a subtotaled figure as the headline income measure a difficult endeavor, it is also potentially quite misleading. For example, consider WorldCom's use of EBITDA (which I have always viewed as a strange measure) as the headline income measure. As the *Financial Times* observed, "The WorldCom scam moved expenses from above EBITDA to below it. . . . Investors need to look at all aspects of performance—not just 'earnings before the bad stuff.'"[3] In the case of the WorldCom scandal, the company defined certain operating cash flows as investing cash flows so that these cash flows were not included in EBITDA for the period—a straightforward bit of misinformation. Further, if these cash flows are capitalized as an asset and subsequently amortized, they will not flow through the headline earnings measure in future periods either. So, the subtotaled income measure can be misleading because of the leeway available in circumventing it. The only measure that is not misleading in this sense is comprehensive income because it includes all items that affect reported performance—thus, a company does not have the leeway to exclude negative items. (Note, however, that to criticize companies for decisions to report only losses below the line is somewhat unfair. An inevitable consequence of conservatism in accounting is that below-the-line losses are more likely than below-the-line gains.)

Comprehensive income is the ultimate bottom line. It is defined under U.S. GAAP as being the change in shareholders' equity (net assets) of a business enterprise over a reporting period from all revenues, expenses, gains, and losses arising from transactions and other events and circumstances from nonowner sources. SFAS No. 130, *Reporting Comprehensive Income*, outlines how comprehensive income should be classified and displayed.[4]

This definition of comprehensive income has one advantage: It is consistent with equity valuation theory. Analysts who use an abnormal earnings model or RIM would not want to ignore a large asset write-off simply because it might be a one-time event. If any item of this character slips through the net, these types of valuation models will not work. The free cash flow model is only consistent with the abnormal earnings model or RIM if the abnormal earnings model has a clean surplus (i.e., if it uses comprehensive income).

---

[3] *Financial Times* editorial (27 January 2002).

[4] A summary of SFAS No. 130 (issued June 1997) can be found at www.fasb.org/st/summary/stsum130.shtml.

Comprehensive income, however, is not a good measure of a company's earnings performance. Comprehensive income cannot sensibly be used in a valuation multiple because it includes all transactions, events, and circumstances (even those that are not ongoing) and thus does not provide the best basis for forecasting.

Designing a New Income Statement

A general problem for the IASB's income statement project is that recognition and measurement is not an objective science. The measurement of the different income statement components is unavoidably subjective and thereby open to different interpretations. Consider the example of AOL Time Warner. According to the company's headline statement in its 2001 financials, the company had normalized EBITDA growth of 18 percent and free cash flow growth in excess of 200 percent, both of which are remarkably good. Careful scrutiny, however, would reveal the reference to a likely future write-off of goodwill:

> On the balance sheet side, SFAS No. 142 [*Goodwill and Other Intangible Assets*] requires goodwill to be revalued.[5] Accordingly, we are expecting to record a one-time, non-cash charge in our income statement for the first quarter of 2002 in the $40–60 billion range to reflect overall market declines since the AOL Time Warner merger was announced in January 2000. The charge will be reflected as the cumulative effect of adopting the change required by this pronouncement, and does not affect the Company's operations.

In my view, this statement contains many "disclaimers." First, the company is "expecting to record a one-time, non-cash charge." Translation: This cost is not relevant to future cash flow. Second, the effect of this charge to the income statement will be "in the $40–60 billion range." Translation: The company is not sure what the magnitude will be; it could be $40 billion or $60 billion, give or take a mere $20 billion. Third, the charge is "to reflect overall market declines since the AOL Time Warner merger was announced in January 2000." Translation: The charge is the result of market fluctuations that have nothing to do with the company, and in terms of relative performance, the charge does not reflect an AOL Time Warner problem because the underlying cause is beyond management control. Finally, "The charge will be reflected as the cumulative effect of adopting the change required by this pronouncement." Translation: The charge is an accounting change, a mere bookkeeping entry; it does not affect the company's operations.

In some ways, this treatment is understandable. The charge clearly should not be reflected in the P/E ratio. It is a one-time charge that is not related to operations per se. Nonetheless, it is a very large recognized loss for the period.

The Pension Cost Issue. How to account for and report pension costs is a major issue, not least because the numbers involved are very large. At the risk of oversimplifying, there are three dimensions to pension cost accounting and two alternative models for representing pension cost in the accounts. The three dimensions are the service cost, the pension obligation, and the pension fund assets. Service cost is basically the same as any other type of employee compensation for a given period. The only difference is that settlement is deferred; otherwise, service cost is the same as wages. The deferral, however, can be for very long periods, which gives rise to a large, difficult-to-estimate pension obligation. The difference between the pension obligation and pension fund assets is the surplus or deficit for the pension plan.

The two alternative models for representing pension cost can be termed the "net, smoothed" model and the "gross, immediate recognition" model. The difference is in the treatment of value changes in the pension plan's obligation and assets. In essence, the "net, smoothed" model allows these changes to flow through the income statement over a long time period because the net cost is amortized over the service life of the employee. In contrast, the "gross, immediate recognition" model "sees through" net pension cost to the various components that are decidedly different in nature, and it reports immediately the value changes in each. For example, all of the return on pension plan assets would be reported as a gain or a loss in the period.

Gains and losses on pension assets and liabilities are not closely related to operating performance and are, to a significant extent, beyond management's control—for example, the value of the pension obligation depends greatly on estimates of mortality rates, interest rates, and so on, which are clearly beyond management's control. And providing pension funding is certainly a noncore activity. But although excluding these pension costs from a sustainable earnings measure might make sense and be widely accepted, completely removing them from the income statement is difficult to justify. Pension assets and obligations clearly meet the definition of assets and liabilities. Pension assets are claims to expected economic benefits, just as the pension liability is an obligation to a transfer of economic benefits.

---

[5] A summary of SFAS No. 142 (issued June 2001) can be found at www.fasb.org/st/summary/stsum142.shtml or see Appendix D of the AIMR proceedings *Closing the Gap between Financial Reporting and Reality* (Charlottesville, VA, 2003: AIMR).

In economic substance, they do not differ from other types of assets and liabilities, which appear on the balance sheet with value changes reported in income.

The IASB is currently proposing a move toward the "gross, immediate recognition" model, which would result in currently unrecognized gains and losses being run through the income statement. The current practice of combining all pension-related items into a single net pension cost is not terribly informative. Net pension cost has different components, some of which are clearly financial in nature and not directly related to the entity's operating activity, such as interest cost and the return on plan assets. When all the components are netted together and run through the income statement, the impact on operating profit can be misleading. A recent Morgan Stanley report calculated the effect on reported operating profit of excluding the recognized income on pension assets.[6] For example, in 2001, the operating profit of DaimlerChrysler would have been reduced by 58 percent, and for Royal Philips Electronics and SAS, the reduction would have been 63 percent and 85 percent, respectively.

Moreover, the expected return-on-assets component of net pension cost can be changed almost at will, meaning that not only is operating profit distorted but the extent of the distortion is somewhat controllable by management. Also, although the four pension cost components could be categorized more accurately by splitting them (say, into operating and financing costs), their interdependence also needs to be reflected. The reason expected return on assets is so controversial is that it is a subjective assumption that flows through the income statement and affects earnings. If the assumption proves to be wrong, the adverse impact on earnings is corrected only imperfectly and only over time. It would be better, surely, to report objective changes in asset values in the period in which they occur and to restrict subjective judgment in profit reporting.

Proposed Format. The objective for the new format of the income statement is to categorize, order, and display information so as to maximize predictive value for comprehensive income and its components. We believe that a useful step in achieving this objective is the disaggregation of total income and expenses into components having different informational properties. One disaggregation is between operating (or "business") and financing activities, and another is based on what we are calling "remeasurements."

---
[6] "European Pensions: A Leaking VAT?" Morgan Stanley (22 May 2002). This report can be found at www.morganstanley.com/im/uk/views/pdfs/leaking_vat.pdf.

An accounting period can include four different types of income and expense. The first type arises on the initial recognition of a transaction or event, such as payment for employee services received. The second type is the consumption of an asset, in the form of amortization or depreciation. The third type arises as a consequence of the passage of time, such as interest income on a bond or dividend income on a stock. The fourth type is a remeasurement, which arises when the value of an asset or a liability changes because the assumptions and estimates that were inputs to the carrying value of that asset or liability are changed.

A remeasurement concerns the estimates of future cash flows and future economic benefits or costs associated with an asset or liability, and it is reflected on the income statement as a one-time charge. That is, the company is moving from one current value to a new current value, from a capitalized number to another capitalized number. Such a change has little, if any, predictive value.

Remeasurements capture many of the items that cause problems when using the income statement to project sustainable performance—for example, it includes goodwill impairment and pension plan actuarial gains and losses, both of which could have a large impact on reported performance but neither of which is obviously useful in predicting future operating performance. Similar conclusions hold for mark-to-market changes on financial instruments and for disposal gains/losses, revaluations, or impairments of PPE.

Exhibit 1 shows in outline form the (provisional) proposed format for a new income statement. The first column reports total income and expenses, and the second and third columns disaggregate the total in order to provide more information to users. The "income before remeasurements" column represents the first three types of income and expense—those generated at initial recognition (e.g., revenues), from consumption of an asset (e.g., depreciation), and through the passage of time (e.g., interest expense). The third column reports the remeasurements.

Before we could begin to redesign the income statement, three questions needed to be answered.

Exhibit 1. Outline of Proposed Format

	Total	Income before Remeasurements	Remeasurements
Business	×××	××	××
Financing	××	×	×
Comprehensive income	××		

First, should we attempt to define separate categories of performance? In our view, such a separation is necessary—for example, pension plan actuarial gains and losses should not appear in the same place as service costs.

Second, if separate performance categories are created, how should they be displayed? The choice is between a single-column format and a matrix. With a single-column format, a sharp distinction would need to be made between items "above the line," such as operating and financing activities, and those below, which would be deemed "nonoperating." For reasons identified earlier, this approach poses problems. For example, when and why would the gain or loss on disposal of property be above or below the line? In contrast, a matrix approach does not require a sharp, difficult-to-draw distinction because the introduction of disaggregated data in the columns allows a more informative display. For example, whereas the "total" column would include the total income and expenses arising on PPE, the disaggregation in the columns would separate depreciation (i.e., the ongoing charge for the consumption of assets) from the more volatile and less predictive income and expenses arising from asset revaluations, impairments, and disposal gains and losses. Moreover, the disaggregated display would highlight the measurement interdependence of these various PPE-related income and expenses. If a company is consistently underdepreciating, this method will cause it to consistently report disposal losses in the "remeasurements" column. Likewise, if the expected return on pension plan assets is overstated in the "income before remeasurements" column, the "remeasurements" column will show consistently poor performance of pension plan assets. The matrix method provides transparency for the inherent subjectivity in measurement.

Third, how can the items in the "remeasurements" column be presented to provide useful information to equity analysts as to company balance sheet risk? For example, if a company does not have a defined-benefit pension plan, no item related to pension cost will be in the "remeasurements" column because no outstanding pension obligation exists. And if a company does not have significant exposure to financial instruments, the fair value changes reported as remeasurements over the period would not be material.

So, our matrix approach shows the balance sheet risk and gives an indication of a company's earnings management and earnings quality in two ways. First, if a company has inherent exposure to unpredictable volatility through balance sheet risk, it will report greater remeasurement amounts. Second, to the extent that management's estimates are unreliable (e.g., the likely settlement amount of provisions), amounts reported in the "income before remeasurements" column will consistently show up in the "remeasurements" column in future periods, as they are revised. In other words, the information in the "remeasurements" column provides feedback information about the sustainability and predictability of the entity's reported performance.

Conclusion

A single, objective measure of earnings cannot be defined in a straightforward, rigorous way. The fundamental problem is one of inherent inconsistency and subjectivity in the measurement of earnings, compounded by increasing amounts of volatility in the income statement. In attempting to devise a new income statement, the IASB is seeking to establish a method that captures the critical facets of earnings and that provides transparency for subjective measurements. If defined by accounting standards, such a measurement could provide the uniformity necessary to make earnings measurements more useful and intelligible to equity analysts.

Question and Answer Session

Richard Barker

Question: To what extent does the new Standard & Poor's (S&P) core earnings measure succeed in segregating nonoperating earnings?

Barker: Segregating nonoperating earnings is difficult to do, and I don't think S&P's measure achieves it. The Institute of Investment Management and Research (IIMR), the former U.K. body (now the U.K. Society of Investment Professionals), attempted to define operating earnings in the early 1990s. In fact, this standard is still quoted in the *Financial Times*. S&P has tried to do precisely the same thing but is coming under heavy criticism. The problem lies in trying to define operating earnings as a single number because a measure of earnings that is a subtotal cannot be defined in a simple, rigorous, objective way. Anyone who claims to have *the* measure is going to attract criticism, as S&P has found with their proposed definition of core earnings. They recently revised their core earnings number and, no doubt, will continue to revise it.

Question: Will the IASB attempt to define a number similar to S&P's core earnings?

Barker: The IASB's approach will likely be limited to just defining the measure that is required by accounting standards and identifying all of the measure's components so that an analyst can find the bits that conform to the in-house definition that his or her firm chooses to develop. We're probably not going to expose ourselves to criticism by claiming that we have developed the one key measure that truly matters.

The problem is that finding the magic number is a search for the Holy Grail. This project has been on the IASB's agenda for decades. A report from the early 1970s by Brian Carsberg, who was then the technical director of the FASB and the predecessor of David Tweedie as the IASB chairman, uses precisely the same language we are currently using regarding the introduction of volatility to the income statement and the need to ameliorate that volatility, as well as the problem of defining earnings separately from comprehensive income. Although many smart people have attempted to deal with this problem over time, it keeps returning to the agenda.

Question: If an objective measure is so difficult to define, what is the best approach?

Barker: The pragmatic approach, as was taken by IIMR, is to identify the headline earnings number—the number chosen as the basis for consistent headline reporting in press releases, P/E ratios, and so on. Analysts would be expected to make their own adjustments to improve the number in a way that's relevant to their own valuation multiples. Such an approach is a reasonable position, but an underlying problem is the perceived need for the number. Why is the number so important? The question leads to the strong implicit assumptions that are made in using P/E ratios, as well as the difficulties created by the underlying subjectivity of the data and the calculation of earnings. A change of mindset is required, and although I think we are seeing this change to some extent, there remains an excessive focus on a single metric of performance.

Question: What process is being followed to achieve global accounting standard convergence?

Barker: In effect, there are two dominant standards boards (the IASB and the FASB), and they have formally agreed (at a joint meeting on 18 September 2002 at the FASB offices in Connecticut) to work together and to converge. They have written and published a formal memorandum of agreement on convergence. The U.S. SEC and the European Community have endorsed it. The two boards will compare their current sets of standards and pick the best of the standards over time. For example, in terms of stock compensation standards, the U.S. standard is the best in the world, but it has a critical flaw. The proposed international standard would solve that critical flaw, and it would be surprising if the U.S. standard didn't come into line with the international standard. But on business combinations, the international community is converging on the U.S. model.

Many of the other major standard setters are about to align with the IASB. The United Kingdom, Germany, France, Australia, and New Zealand all have representative status on the IASB board and will adopt international standards starting in 2005. Canada and Japan remain uncommitted to accepting the international standards. Canada's interests fall between the international standards and the U.S. standards, and the ideal solution for Canada would be convergence of the two. Japan will probably be slower in achieving convergence with the international standards and the U.S. standards, but such convergence is probably inevitable.

So, convergence is an active phenomenon, and the IASB and the FASB will be working together on future projects. When new agenda items appear from now on, we hope there won't be two different solutions. Eventually, we can expect that two sets of standards will exist that are virtually indistinguishable.

Question: Are the IASB and the FASB bracing for criticism from the U.S. Congress on such issues as employee stock options?

Barker: Enron and other recent financial scandals have helped enormously in a few ways. First, the controversy has raised the profile of accounting regulations and has caused Congress to turn face on such accounting issues as stock compensation. (Patricia McConnell described this issue particularly well during her presentation.)[1] The political climate has changed but so has the perception of global accounting standards and the need for the FASB to work with the IASB.

Question: As of 2005, should we expect any major developments in derivatives and inflation accounting?

Barker: Regarding the latter, the answer depends on future inflation. When inflation was rampant in the 1970s and early 1980s, inflation accounting was a big deal, even though it was inherently difficult to do. The conceptual difficulties associated with inflation accounting have not gone away, but inflation is no longer a major concern. If high inflation returns, the subject will be back on the agenda, but for the present, there is little enthusiasm to address it. If the fair value method is used more often in financial statements, the issues associated with inflation accounting will be reduced because marking to market on the balance sheet captures inflation gains. To a significant degree, the problem is one of historical cost accounting.

Motivation exists to move toward fair valuation of all financial instruments, including derivatives, but it is an immensely difficult thing to do. Fair value is probably the right answer in terms of the standard setters' conceptual framework and for many valuation models. (A free cash flow model or an abnormal earnings model often contains an implicit assumption that net financial assets have zero net present value and do not generate wealth for the company being valued, but rather that wealth is generated from a company's operating assets. Of course, this assumption is true in practice only if the financial instruments are held at fair value.)

Question: Why is a conversion to fair value accounting for all financial assets so difficult to do?

Barker: Fair value has several complexities. For one thing, it is difficult to explain. For example, if a company values its liabilities at fair value, it has to change the value of its debt on the balance sheet whenever its market value changes, which introduces the entity's own credit risk into its financial statements. The reduction in fair value from one period to the next would show up as a gain on the income statement. Consequently, if the entity is in financial trouble and its debt is downgraded, the result is, at least to the extent of its debt remeasurement, a positive influence on the entity's bottom line. This appears counterintuitive at first sight, and much education needs to be done for fair value accounting to work.

A fundamental problem is that the measurement of fair value and the associated measurement of profit are especially difficult for financial institutions. This matters not least because the source of value creation for these entities is financial instruments and because the fair value model is not applied comprehensively to all financial instruments. The IASB has been deliberating with insurance companies about this problem for quite a long time now, and the debate is ongoing. The IASB's recognition and measurement standard on financial instruments (IAS No. 39, *Financial Instruments: Recognition and Measurement*) is at the center of active and ongoing discussions with banks and other institutions.[2]

Question: Can you give us the principles behind the pension cost, employee stock option, and goodwill impairment accounting that the IASB is likely to adopt and the standards that are likely to be proposed?

Barker: The final decisions have not yet been made, so my answer represents only my personal perspective.

The standard regarding goodwill is likely, in essence, to follow the U.S. standard in that at an acquisition, the entity will recognize goodwill on the balance sheet and review it annually for impairment. This approach is conceptually correct, but it has unavoidable measurement challenges. Goodwill is intrinsically difficult to value, and the IASB's approach is likely to emphasize not just the principles behind the valuation but also the disclosure of the entity's assumptions made in the valuation. I think this approach is promising in terms of maximizing information for users.

Compensation in the form of employee stock options is likely to be expensed on a grant-date, fair value basis, but after the grant date, changes in the fair value would not affect the income statement. Once stock compensation is issued, the employees become owners, and just as changes in share prices do not flow through the income statement, changes in the employee's stock option prices should not flow

---

[1] Please see Patricia McConnell's presentation in this proceedings.

[2] A summary of IAS No. 39 (issued January 2001) can be found at www.iasb.org.uk/cmt/0001.asp?n=983&s=6819601&sc={442AEE50-1220-414B-B17F-C71C6F611988}&sd=407997578.

through the income statement either.

As for pension costs, it is possible that the international standard will move closer to the U.K. standard, which is immediate recognition. An entity recognizes the service cost when an employee is first employed and then recognizes any subsequent changes in the value of the pension obligation and the value of pension assets through the income statement as they occur—no smoothing. In my view, this approach greatly improves transparency and economic relevance in business reporting.

Question: What is your opinion of conservative accounting?

Barker: My main concern with conservative accounting is that it is not truly conservative; rather, it creates distortion. Suppose you have a conservative accounting policy and you write off all assets and take all losses as soon as possible. The result is an overstatement of return on capital in future periods. You have to recognize income and expenses at some stage, and conservatism recognizes the expenses sooner and the income later. Because this approach reduces your asset base and your future amortizable amount, it increases your income and reduces your capital, thus increasing return on capital. Furthermore, the calculation of return on capital has no mechanism for correcting this problem. So, if you write off assets conservatively, the consequence is persistent overstatement of return on capital in future periods, a fundamental distortion. Return on capital in accounting is significantly different from an economic measure, such as the internal rate of return, and no simple relationship between accounting return and economic return exists.

The more conservative the accounting, the more inflated the return on capital will be relative to the actual true economic return, which is worrisome. For example, if return on capital is used in an RIM, it measures economic profit in the period; the more conservative the accounting, the more misleading the economic profit number will be.

Question: What do you think about IAS No. 19, *Employee Benefits*,[3] and SFAS No. 87, *Employers' Accounting for Pensions*?[4]

---

[3] A summary of IAS No. 19 (issued January 1999) can be found at www.iasc.org.uk/cmt/0001.asp?s=4500263&sc={C8EEFA3C-1199-4595-87EA-D863239E786E}&sd=655432057&n=962.

[4] A summary of SFAS No. 87 (issued December 1985) can be found at www.fasb.org/st/summary/stsum87.shtml or see Appendix A of the AIMR proceedings *Closing the Gap between Financial Reporting and Reality* (Charlottesville, VA, 2003: AIMR).

Barker: We have heard a lot about IAS No. 19 and SFAS No. 87 at this conference. If you did not follow everything that has been discussed, I sympathize with you. I suspect the reason for some confusion is that the two standards are not intuitively easy to understand. They are similar, and I think that both generate opaque and potentially misleading reporting. The IASB is undertaking a project to revise IAS No. 19, and I would expect to see this follow an immediate recognition model, along similar lines as Financial Reporting Standard (FRS) 17, the standard that has caused so much excitement in the United Kingdom. I think that an FRS 17-type solution is consistent with the conceptual framework of both the IASB and the FASB and would greatly enhance transparent reporting of pension costs.

Quality of Earnings: Avoiding the Accounting Landmines

Patricia A. McConnell
Senior Managing Director
Bear, Stearns & Company Inc.
New York City

> Recent corporate controversies have highlighted the link between accounting practices and varying levels of earnings quality. Earnings quality is critical to the valuation of a company, but in the absence of financial transparency, analysts must examine financial statements to find the truth about a company's quality of earnings. To avoid serious valuation errors, analysts need to dodge the accounting landmines buried in the areas of pension cost, employee stock option expense, and revenue recognition.

"Quality of earnings" directly affects the valuation of a company, and the accounting treatment associated with three high-profile issues—pensions, employee stock options, and revenue recognition—directly affects the quality of earnings. Investor concerns about corporate accounting reliability have mounted with each newly revealed corporate debacle. Therefore, to avoid accounting landmines under current U.S. GAAP, analysts must carefully examine the accounting choices a company makes when constructing its financial statements and assess the effect of those choices on its earnings quality.

Pensions

A financial media frenzy has turned the spotlight on pensions—namely, the potentially huge liability that pension plans represent for companies and the impact that funding obligations will have on corporate earnings and cash flow.

Types of Plans. In the United States, companies use either a defined-benefit or defined-contribution plan or a combination of the two. As the name suggests, in a defined-contribution plan, the company's contribution to the plan is defined in the plan agreement. Once the contribution is made, the company has no further obligation to the employee. The investment risk falls entirely on employees and retirees. Defined-benefit plans, on the other hand, define the benefit that employees will receive at retirement. The specific retirement benefit that is promised is a form of deferred compensation, and all of the investment risk falls on the company. The company is not off the hook until the employee dies. Accordingly, the accounting and funding for this benefit are based on a very long-term view of the employee's working career and retirement and are the source of the current controversy.

Accounting Theory. For defined-benefit plans, the pension benefit that an employee "earns" by working during the current year is referred to as service cost. A company calculates service cost based on the pension formula in the plan documents. The company forecasts how long the employee is likely to live—how long he or she will be in retirement—and thus need to receive the additional benefit earned in the current year. The company then discounts to present value the stream of these benefits that the employee is expected to receive during retirement. This present value amount is service cost, a compensation expense, just like an employee's paycheck. The only difference is that the employee does not receive this compensation (plus interest) until his or her retirement years. In effect, the employee is lending that amount to the company until he or she retires.

The theory behind pension accounting and funding is rather simple. If a company were to contribute to its pension fund each year an amount equal to that year's service cost and invest that contribution in an asset, or pool of assets, that earns the same rate as the discount rate used to calculate the service cost, then when the employee retired, there would be sufficient assets in the fund from which to pay the promised retirement benefit until the employee died. The accounting tries to capture this relatively straightforward approach.

Unfortunately, life is rarely as simple as theory. In the real world, interest rates and asset returns change year to year and employees retire earlier or later than expected and live longer than or not as long as expected. So, pension accounting is complicated by rules about how to: forecast the benefits to be paid during retirement; discount future benefits to present value; record the assets in the pension fund; calculate interest expense on the pension obligation; estimate the return on fund assets; and deal with all the changes in the assumptions and estimates used to calculate pension cost and the pension obligation in prior years. The number that results is included in the income statement—as net pension cost. But because of all the assumptions and estimates that go into the calculation of net pension *cost*, the net pension cost number may actually be net pension *income*, much to many people's amazement.

Pension Cost Components. Net pension cost, or net pension income, has six components. The first component is service cost, or the deferred compensation that the employee earns by working during the current year, as I discussed previously.

Interest on the pension obligation is the second component. Remember, to calculate service cost, the benefits to be paid in the future are discounted to their present value. The service cost related to an employee accumulates over the employee's working career and becomes the pension obligation. The obligation grows larger because of the passage of time. I like to think of the pension obligation as a giant zero-coupon bond owed to the employees. A zero-coupon bond accretes interest over its term to maturity, and the interest accretes more rapidly as the maturity date approaches. The interest component of pension cost works the same way. The interest component of pension cost is the increase in the value of the pension obligation that accumulates with the passage of time.

The third component of pension cost is the one that is causing all the controversy today in the United States—expected return on plan assets—and I will return to this topic later.

The next three components are amortization numbers: amortization of prior service cost, amortization of net gains or losses, and amortization of the transition amount.

Prior service cost arises when a company decides to increase the retirement benefit to which employees or retirees are entitled, giving them credit for years they have already worked, which is referred to as prior service credit. Although this prior service credit immediately increases the pension obligation, immediate recognition is not required under GAAP. The increase in the pension obligation arising because of a prior service credit is not expensed and is not recorded on the balance sheet when granted. Rather, it is viewed as a benefit that employees will earn over the future course of their working careers in the future. The increase in the pension obligation as a result of a prior service credit is deferred and amortized over the remaining service life of active employees or, if it relates to retirees, over the remaining life of retirees.

The second amortization number is amortization of net deferred gains or losses, which arises from changes in the assumptions used to calculate the pension obligation and the actual return on fund assets being more or less than estimated return. Thus, it is intimately related to the return-on-assets component that I will discuss shortly.

The third amortization number is amortization of the transition amount, a historical artifact of Statement of Financial Accounting Standards (SFAS) No. 87, *Employers' Accounting for Pensions*, which was implemented between 1985 and 1987. This number represents the amortization of the amount by which the company was over- or underfunded at the date it adopted the new accounting rule (that is, the difference between the plan obligation and the plan assets at the inception of the new accounting rule). Under the transition provisions of the accounting rule, the amount by which the plan was over- or underfunded at adoption was not recorded on the balance sheet immediately. Rather, it was deferred and amortized through net pension cost over the remaining service life of active employees.[1] Think of the amortization of the transition amount as the amortization of the cumulative effect of an accounting change. This transition amortization is about to evaporate and will never be seen again.

■ *Expected Return on Plan Assets*. The return-on-plan-assets component of pension cost is the *expected* return on plan assets. It is calculated by multiplying an expected long-term rate of return by the "value of plan assets." By applying an expected long-term rate of return to the value of plan assets, companies can smooth out the peaks and valleys of market returns over time, thus showing less deviation from year to year in net pension cost on the income statement.

---

[1]Although the service life of active employees is 15 years, on average in corporate America, the service career is much longer for some companies and much shorter for others; it also expands and contracts over time because of layoffs or the hiring of younger workers.

The value of plan assets used can be either the fair value of the plan assets at the beginning of the year, adjusted for benefits paid or contributions made during the year, or a moving average of the fair value of plan assets for a three-, four-, or five-year period. Few companies have chosen to use the fair value at the beginning of the year because doing so would, to some extent, negate the smoothing effect that results from using a constant expected rate of return. Instead, most companies use the three-, four-, or five-year moving average to calculate the dollar amount of expected return. Companies in the aerospace industry, for instance, use a three-year moving average, but many companies in other industries use a five-year moving average.

Reports in the financial media have expressed concern about the expected rates of return that have been used by U.S. companies in calculating their pension cost. For companies in the S&P 500 Index, the median expected rate of return has been around 9 percent since 1987, when SFAS No. 87 was implemented. A wide range of expected rates of return exists, from a low of 6 percent to a high of 11.5 percent, but the median rate generally stays around 9 percent. In some years, it may be slightly lower or higher, perhaps because of the changing mix of companies in the S&P 500. The expected rate is intended to reflect the long-term rate of return that the company, its fund managers, actuaries, and auditors expect the mix of assets in the plan to earn over the duration of the pension obligation.

Thus, the stock market's lousy performance in the past three years does not necessarily mean that companies will change their expectations of what they expect debt and equity securities and real estate to earn over the long term. The accounting rule itself does not necessitate that companies lower their expected rate-of-return assumptions. The expected rate of return that companies disclose is a weighted-average rate. So, if the mix of assets in a company's pension portfolio changes, the weighted-average rate (the expected rate of return) will also change. For example, the expected rate of return for a company may decline in 2002 because as equity values decline and bond values increase, if companies are not actively rebalancing their portfolios, a different weighted-average expected rate of return will result.

Because of such smoothing effects, pension cost did not spike dramatically when U.S. equity markets began to decline in 2000 or 2001. The moving average of plan assets—to which companies were applying the expected rate of return—was still rising from the tremendous gains in both the stock and bond markets of the late 1990s. Thus, smoothing protected companies on the upside and kept pension income from decreasing dramatically or pension cost from rising dramatically. After three years of negative stock market returns, however, companies are on the downhill side of the smoothing mechanism. By 2003, they will begin to feel the effects of the stock market downturn on the moving average of the plan assets. And just as smoothing managed to stretch out high expected returns while the market declined, smoothing will have a similar effect on the other side; smoothing will stretch out increasing pension cost and decreasing pension income. For a number of years to come, even if the markets are flat or begin to rise, recent market performance will be reflected in the moving average of the value of pension plan assets.

Amortization of the Difference between Expected and Actual Return. The difference between the expected return and the actual return on plan assets is related to the amortized gain or loss component of pension cost, to which I referred earlier. If the plan assets outperform (underperform) the expected rate, recognition of the resulting gain (loss) is deferred. The gains and losses are netted together and eventually amortized.

Again, SFAS No. 87 allows for substantial smoothing. Companies have two alternatives. One alternative is to amortize the pension plan's net deferred gain or loss on a systematic and rational basis, which might be straight line over the remaining service period of existing employees. For example, the General Electric Company amortizes its plan's net deferred gain or loss over the remaining service life of its active employees, which appears to be around 20 years.

The other alternative is to wait to amortize the net deferred gain or loss until it becomes quite large. The theory supporting this alternative is that the market is self-correcting and reverts to the mean over the long term, so the plan assets should earn the long-term expected rate of return without the company having to amortize the plan's gains or losses. But to "scoundrel proof" the rule, the FASB added a provision that requires the net deferred gain or loss to be amortized when it becomes so big as to be embarrassing. "Big" is defined as more than 10 percent of plan assets or more than 10 percent of plan liabilities, whichever is greater. If the amount exceeds the threshold, the excess amount has to be amortized over the remaining service life of the active employees. Clearly, amortization of the net deferred gains and losses contributes to the smoothing that occurs in determining net pension cost.

Because the net deferred gains or losses on plan assets are ultimately amortized, the debate about whether the expected long-term rate of return is too high or low is somewhat misguided, at least for long-term investors. Over a market cycle, a company will report in net income the actual return on its pension plan assets through the combination of the expected return component in pension cost and the amortization of the amount earned in excess of the expected return or the amount of the expected return shortfall. Earnings will thus reflect exactly the amount that the plan assets earned. The use of the expected rate of return simply smooths the peaks and valleys of market performance.

■ *Unfunded Accumulated Benefit Obligation*. The deferral and amortization model for calculating net pension cost (income) under SFAS No. 87 can result in a company not recording on its balance sheet the true amount by which its pension plan is under- or overfunded. This problem can occur because the company has net deferred gains or losses in its pension plan, unamortized prior service cost, or an unamortized transition amount. Thus, the actual economic position of the company's pension plan is not shown on its balance sheet.

In the United States, the Employee Retirement Income Security Act of 1974 (ERISA) guarantees retirees defined benefits in the case of the bankruptcy of the sponsoring company and gives the Pension Benefit Guarantee Corporation (PBGC), which oversees ERISA, a priority claim in bankruptcy for assets necessary to satisfy the unfunded pension obligation. The FASB did not want to issue a pension accounting standard that would result in a company's legal liability in bankruptcy not being recorded on its balance sheet, but it did want a standard that allowed smoothing of pension cost in net income through deferral and amortization.

To accomplish both objectives, the FASB created the minimum pension liability adjustment. Pension cost is calculated using the deferral and amortization mechanism, as already explained. At the end of each year, the company must also calculate its minimum pension liability. The minimum pension liability approximates a company's legal obligation under ERISA if the company were to declare bankruptcy. The minimum pension liability is calculated as the difference between a company's accumulated pension obligation (ABO) and the fair value of its plan assets on the balance sheet date.

The ABO is calculated without reference to salary inflation, so it is lower than the normal ongoing pension obligation used to calculate net pension cost when the plan benefit formula is based on employee compensation levels. For S&P 500 companies in the aggregate, the ABO represents about 85 percent of the ongoing benefit obligation. An unfunded ABO represents the minimum pension liability that must appear on a company's balance sheet. The company compares the minimum pension liability with the pension liability it has recorded on the balance sheet as a result of the normal deferral and amortization mechanism. If the pension liability recorded is not at least equal to the unfunded ABO, the company has to record an additional pension liability.

As everyone knows, on the balance sheet, assets must equal liabilities plus equity. When a company records an unfunded ABO, the company's liabilities increase. To keep its balance sheet in balance, the company takes a charge directly to a component of equity that the FASB has dubbed "other comprehensive income." This adjustment for the unfunded ABO never has a direct impact on a company's reported earnings. If the ABO becomes larger (smaller), a company can keep increasing (reducing) the liability and reducing (increasing) equity. In a sense, the adjustment is relevant only if the company is close to, or actually in, bankruptcy. The ABO simply approximates the PBGC's claim on the company in the event of bankruptcy.

Cash Flow Implications of Defined-Benefit Plans. Pension cost has no effect on a company's cash flow. In fact, SFAS No. 87 is not considered an acceptable methodology for calculating the contribution to a pension plan. ERISA, however, does contain a funding requirement. Companies tend to make the contributions to their pension plans at an amount between the ERISA minimum requirement and the maximum amount deductible under the U.S. Internal Revenue Service code.

Under ERISA, companies have to make an additional deficit-reduction contribution when they become underfunded. If a company has a funding ratio (assets as a percent of liabilities) of less than 90 percent, it is considered to be underfunded. If the ratio has been less than 90 percent for two consecutive years over the past three years, the company has to make a deficit-reduction contribution when that funding ratio falls below 80 percent. In other words, as long as the funding ratio is 80 percent or above and has been 90 percent or above in two out of the past three years, no additional contribution is necessary. Clearly, a lot of smoothing is incorporated into the requirement for an additional deficit-reduction contribution. Even though some companies are likely to have to make additional contributions in 2003, the contributions will not be particularly large. And many companies will not have to make a contribution because their funding ratio has been higher than 90 percent until recently.

Despite the poor performance of the stock market in recent years, the situation with pensions is not as dire as it might appear. The U.S. Congress and PBGC have no desire to force a company into bankruptcy because it cannot make its required contributions under ERISA in a particular year. Indeed, establishing a funding mechanism to keep companies solvent until the market rebounds is in everybody's interest—shareholders, retirees, employees, and so on.

Employee Stock Options

Employee stock options are an enormous accounting problem in the United States. Outside the United States, options are less of a problem, but the accounting rules for them are nonexistent in most jurisdictions. The International Accounting Standards Board (IASB) is working to make the expensing of options using the fair value method a mandatory requirement for companies following International Accounting Standards (IAS). I believe that, in the not too distant future, the FASB will also make the fair value method of expensing employee stock options mandatory in the United States.

Accounting Methods. From an accounting perspective, the question of whether employee stock options represent a compensation expense is moot. Fifty years ago, the accounting standard setters of the time concluded, in an Accounting Series Release, that options given to employees were a compensation expense.[2] Accountants have agreed that options given to employees represent a compensation expense, and the accounting debate for the past 50 years has centered around how to measure that expense. In 1972, the Accounting Principles Board (APB) issued Opinion No. 25, *Accounting for Stock Issued to Employees*, which requires the use of the intrinsic value method to measure the compensation expense of options given to employees. Under the intrinsic value method, cost is measured as the difference between the fair value of the underlying stock and the exercise price of the option at the date of grant. The appeal of this method is that if the exercise price is set at the market price at the grant date, the intrinsic value, or compensation cost, is zero. In the rare case that the intrinsic value at the date of grant is greater than zero, it is expensed over the option's vesting period.

The motivation for issuing a rule requiring the use of the intrinsic value method was to prevent companies from issuing in-the-money options to employees without taking a charge to earnings, an abuse that was rampant in the 1960s. But in 1972, when APB No. 25 was issued, Fischer Black and Myron Scholes had not yet published their seminal theory on option valuation.[3] Consequently, the idea of calculating option value using an option-pricing model was too avant-garde to be adopted by the accounting profession at that time.

In the early 1990s, the FASB proposed replacing the intrinsic value method with the fair value method for determining the cost of employee stock option compensation. Under the fair value method, the option is valued at the date of grant using an option-pricing model and that value is charged to compensation expense over the vesting period. But the FASB got into trouble with the U.S. Congress for proposing to eliminate the intrinsic value method. The FASB, an independent, not-for-profit organization, is not supposed to be subject to political influence, but the U.S. Congress threatened to put the FASB out of business if it eliminated the intrinsic value method. Members of Congress were persuaded by their constituents that this method had given the United States the world lead in technology and the lowest cost of capital in the world. As a result, the final version of SFAS No. 123 permits companies to use either the intrinsic value or fair value method.

Until the summer of 2002, only two companies in the S&P 500 Index had elected to expense options using the fair value method—the Boeing Company and Winn-Dixie Stores. Since then, however, a number of companies have announced their intention to adopt the fair value method. Bear Stearns has compiled a list of 192 companies that have announced their intention to adopt the fair value method.[4] Only a handful of the 192 are technology, or "new economy," companies. For the sake of regaining credibility with the investment community, companies such as the General Electric Company and the Coca-Cola Company have decided they are willing to adopt the fair value method. At Bear Stearns, we believe the FASB will mandate the use of the fair value method by 2004 or 2005.

As mentioned earlier, the IASB has issued an exposure draft that would require companies following its standards to use the fair value method.[5] In June 2002, the European Commission adopted a directive requiring most publicly traded European companies to adopt IAS by 2005. Publicly traded European companies that currently follow U.S. GAAP have until 2007. If all goes according to plan, most public com-

---

[2] Committee on Accounting Procedure, "Compensation Involved in Stock Option and Stock Purchase Plans," *Accounting Research Bulletin No. 43*, Chapter 13B (1952).

[3] Fischer Black and Myron Scholes, "The Pricing of Options and Corporate Liabilities," *Journal of Political Economy* (1973):637–659.

[4] Bear, Stearns & Company, Inc., "Employee Stock Option Accounting: New Developments," *Accounting Issues* (28 February 2003).

[5] The exposure draft "ED 2 Share-based Payment" was released on 7 November 2002 and was available for public comment until 7 March 2003. It could become effective by the end of 2003 as a voluntary standard and then adopted as a rule in Europe in 2005. The proposal may be viewed at www.iasc.org.uk.

panies in Europe will be using the fair value method of accounting for options by 2005. We believe the FASB is likely to try to eliminate the use of the intrinsic value method in the United States in the name of international harmonization and convergence to the highest level of accounting standards. If the intrinsic value method remains as a choice under GAAP, the European Commission might complain to the World Trade Organization about predatory accounting practices in the United States, because, after all, the U.S. Congress credited the intrinsic value method with giving the United States the world lead in technology and the world's lowest cost of capital (even though the party is now over for technology companies).

Effect on Earnings Quality. The question about how the fair value method of measuring employee stock option expense will affect earnings has provoked much debate. Fortunately, in SFAS No. 123, the FASB had the foresight to require that companies disclose, in a footnote, what their earnings would have been had they used the fair value method, and this disclosure has appeared in financial statements since 1995. Based on 2001 footnote disclosures, we estimate that the aggregate earnings per share (EPS) of companies in the S&P 500 would have been lower by more than 20 percent if they had been required to expense the fair value of options. This estimate is distorted, however, by the fact that in 2001, the companies in the S&P 500 had unusually low earnings—the result of a number of large impairment charges, particularly those related to goodwill. On a more normalized basis, the switch to fair value expensing should reduce a company's EPS by 10 to 12 percent.

This estimate may still seem high, but when companies actually have to take this charge to earnings, they will likely become more frugal in their use of employee stock options. History has shown that when companies do not have to account for a cost, they do not control it well. Once companies have to account for options, more-sensible compensation decisions will result. Companies will grant fewer options, and the number of employees entitled to options will decline as well. Therefore, the effect on companies' reported earnings (as a result of switching to the fair value method) may not be as negative as the pro forma disclosures suggest.

Revenue Recognition

Even though increasing pension cost and employee stock option compensation expense are matters of great concern in today's market, the most important line item in most income statements is still revenue. Historically, most financial debacles have been caused by poor revenue recognition practices. The fundamental principle governing revenue recognition is simple. Revenue should not be recognized by a company until (1) the earnings process is complete and (2) collectability is reasonably assured. But improper interpretation of this simple principle has tainted the reputations of many companies in the United States and has caused investors to lose a lot of money.

Question of Fraud. Overstating revenue by recording revenue fictitiously or prematurely is clearly fraudulent, but such cases are not always immediately apparent in financial statements. For example, companies can record sales to nonexistent customers, and an analyst has no way of knowing which customers are real and which are not. Or consider another scenario in which a company has an order from a legitimate, creditworthy customer. The company has the inventory in the warehouse but cannot get it on a truck and out the door by the stroke of midnight at the end of the quarter (the end of the accounting period). Under the rules of the U.S. legal system, if the company keeps its books open until morning when the truck is loaded, the management of that company will share the same jail cell with the management of the company that booked revenue to a fictitious client. Discovering this type of behavior through financial statement analysis is virtually impossible.

Other customer arrangements created specifically to manipulate revenue recognition can be even more complicated. Say a company has an arrangement with a client to deliver a number of different products and services under a single contract. For example, when a customer signs a contract with a mobile phone company for 24 months of service at $40 per month and receives a free phone, how does the contractor recognize that revenue? Does the company recognize all the revenue immediately or does it allocate the revenue over the contract period? Or does it recognize some immediately, when the customer receives the phone, and some later, when the phone service is provided? If the latter, how should the payments received from the customer be allocated between the sale of the phone and the provision of the phone service?

The principle of revenue recognition holds simply that companies should recognize revenue when the earnings process is complete and collectibility is assured, but a great deal of debate surrounds the definition of "complete." And whether a percentage-of-completion revenue recognition methodology can be applied to the service portion of a contract is even more controversial. The FASB's Emerging Issues

Task Force (EITF) is working to provide guidance on these and other issues.[6]

EITF Issue No. 00-21. A good example is EITF Issue No. 00-21 (EITF 00-21), "Accounting for Revenue Arrangements with Multiple Deliverables." If enacted, EITF 00-21 will have a far-reaching (and unpredictable) effect on revenue recognition in the United States. EITF 00-21 addresses when and how individual elements (products, services, and/or rights to use assets, as well as performance at different points in time or over different periods of time) of a multiple-element contract should be accounted for separately. For example, in its third quarter 2002 income statement, Perot Systems Corporation announced that if it applied the tentative conclusions of EITF 00-21, the company would have to record adjustments that would reduce EPS through 31 December 2002 by 25 cents to 35 cents. Third quarter 2002 EPS was 17 cents per share (diluted). Perot Systems also stated that the adoption of EITF 00-21 would reduce EPS by roughly 6 cents in 2003. Obviously, the impact of EITF 00-21 could be substantial, particularly for companies in the wireless industry whose contracts deal with delivery of a tangible asset, such as a cell phone, and provision of the wireless service.

---
[6] See also Patricia A. McConnell, "The Current and Future State of Financial Reporting," in *Closing the Gap between Financial Reporting and Reality* (Charlottesville, VA, 2003: AIMR):60–67.

An earlier revenue recognition standard, Staff Accounting Bulletin (SAB) 101, issued by the U.S. SEC in 1999, clearly states that the SEC does not believe that percentage-of-completion accounting using costs incurred to date as the performance measure is acceptable for service contracts. Under EITF 00-21, Perot Systems would no longer be able to use percentage-of-completion accounting and would have to use a straight-line revenue recognition method. If EITF 00-21 is enacted, the overall situation will be confusing because, in some cases, companies will have to restate their earnings and, in this market environment, sorting out the different quality levels of revenue recognition will be difficult.

Conclusion

The recent corporate controversies surrounding the accounting treatment for pensions, employee stock option plans, and revenue recognition have demonstrated the extent to which accounting practices are linked to varying levels of earnings quality. Complete financial transparency will probably never exist, so analysts have no choice but to decipher the financial statements they are given to discover the truth about a company's quality of earnings. To achieve accurate valuations, analysts have to avoid the accounting landmines primarily, but not exclusively, relating to pension cost, employee stock option expense, and revenue recognition.

Question and Answer Session

Patricia A. McConnell

Question: How many S&P 500 companies have defined-benefit plans and how many have defined-contribution plans? Can employees switch back and forth between the two types of plans?

McConnell: Our estimate is that 360 of the S&P 500 companies have defined-benefit pension plans, and almost all of the S&P 500 companies have defined-contribution plans. In the United States, 401(k) regulations allow employees to contribute a portion of their income (pretax) to a 401(k) plan. These plans are sponsored by the employer, but the employer does not necessarily have to make any contributions to the plan. Some companies make matching contributions, but others do not. In many companies, employees are covered by both a defined-benefit plan, to which the employer makes contributions, and a defined-contribution plan, to which only the employee makes contributions. Employees do not switch back and forth between them but are usually covered by either one plan or the other or both.

Question: How solvent are companies that have experienced huge downsizings? For example, the earnings base of the automotive industry has become unbalanced compared with its retired work force, so are downsized companies particularly at risk because of their defined-contribution plans?

McConnell: As a result of ERISA and because the downsizings that occurred in the automotive industry in the late 1970s and early 1980s were bigger than the ones occurring now, we believe most of the automotive industry's problems are behind it. In some companies, the number of retirees equals or exceeds the number of employees, but as retirees die, the situation will change. With a smaller work force, there will be fewer new retirees replacing those that die. The companies' obligations to retirees will begin to decline. The media like to quote the staggering dollar amount of the pension deficit at General Motors Corporation (GM), but in reality, GM's funding ratio fell below 90 percent last year for the first time in 12 years. The company is fairly well funded as far as pension plans go. GM is a huge company with a lot of retirees, but at the moment, the size of GM's pension deficit does not present the company with a solvency issue.

Question: Is it too simplistic to say that a company has a pension problem simply because the company downsized?

McConnell: Yes, it is too simplistic. Terminating employees can actually reduce a pension problem, not make it worse. In the United States, pension benefits are typically determined by an employee's compensation at or around retirement age. The calculation of the obligation starts with the employee's current level of compensation and forecasts the employee's compensation level at retirement. If the employee is terminated, his or her retirement benefits will be based, if the employee is vested, on what the employee earned when he or she was terminated. The obligation is thus reduced by the amount that the employer must accrue for salary inflation until the employee's expected retirement. And if the employee is not vested, the entire benefit obligation to the employee is wiped out!

Question: Is it a necessity to keep the required rate of return on pension assets high and thereby stop mature pension schemes from rebalancing toward bonds to better reflect their liabilities? Is the accounting standard actually driving the liability mix in pension schemes?

McConnell: The pension obligation is discounted at the yield on high-quality (AA) corporate bonds, which is different from the rate-of-return assumption on plan assets. Plan assets are measured at fair value for determining whether the plan is over- or underfunded. This measurement has nothing to do with the expected rate of return on plan assets used to calculate net pension cost. The expected return assumption in the short term does drive the company's pension cost or income. Over the long term, however, the actual return on plan assets drives earnings because the difference between the actual and expected return must be amortized and included in pension cost. Certain actuaries spend their entire careers determining the appropriate asset mix for pension plans. Generally, a plan will hold bonds in an amount sufficient to have enough liquidity to pay the retiree benefits in the short term. The assets that are meant to cover the pension obligation in the long term are invested in equities, where higher growth is expected. This mix is considered to be beneficial to shareholders because the higher the return on the contributions put into the pension plan, the lower the contributions have to be in the future.

Question: What is the impact of lower interest rates on the value of the liability on the balance sheet and the net pension cost on the income statement?

McConnell: The impact of lower interest rates on pension cost increases the service cost component of pension cost because it is discounted at the AA corporate bond yield. But the service cost component is miniscule compared with the other components of pension cost. The lower discount rate also results in a higher pension obligation, which affects the interest cost component of pension cost. The rule of thumb is that for every 25-bp decline in interest rates, the interest cost increases by 5 percent. So, falling interest rates will also contribute to increased pension cost next year. On the balance sheet, the ABO is discounted at the current yield on long-term bonds, so as interest rates fall, the ABO increases. The ABO is then compared with the fair value of the plan assets at the balance sheet date, measured on a mark-to-market basis. With the decline in the stock market and in interest rates, the potential for having an unfunded ABO has increased significantly. As a result, quite a few minimum liability adjustments with offsetting charges to equity are likely to occur.

Question: What is your opinion of Financial Reporting Standard (FRS) 17, S&P "core earnings," and other methods that remove pension cost smoothing? What are accounting boards doing to address these issues?

McConnell: One of the key problems with pensions in the United States is that the current accounting standard (SFAS No. 87) nets all of the pension cost components into a single number. Service cost, interest cost, return on plan assets, and amortization are all netted together and treated as one compensation cost. As a compensation cost, it is part of labor cost. If the company is a manufacturing organization, the pension cost finds its way into cost of goods sold on the balance sheet. So, during the 1990s, when about half of the 360 companies that had defined-benefit plans were reporting net pension income, their pension cost was actually reducing their cost of goods sold.

Even more troubling is that this net pension income was indirectly the result of stock market gains. Analysts put a normal operating multiple on what were essentially stock market gains because they did not recognize that the stock market gains were responsible for improving the margins. A multiple larger than 1 should not be placed on a stock market gain. Consider, for example, that although about 12 percent of Lucent Technologies' operating income came from net pension income, analysts were putting a technology multiple on total operating income. In my view, Lucent's earnings were of poor quality and should not have had a technology multiple. In 2003, when many companies will again have net pension cost because of stock market losses, the resulting quality of earnings will be equally poor. And those earnings shouldn't get an operating income multiple either. They should get a multiple of around 1. If the accountants had disaggregated net pension cost, as FRS 17 states should be done, analysts would have recognized that each of the operating income components was of a different quality.

In our report on the operating income of the S&P 500, we adjust operating income (defined as earnings before interest and taxes) to remove all components of pension cost, except service cost. On this basis, our adjusted operating income of the S&P 500 would have been lower than reported by approximately 2.3 percent in 2001 and 3 percent in 2000. The difference suggests that, all else being equal, the operating earnings of the S&P 500 were of a higher quality in 2001 because they were less affected by stock market gains.[1]

Question: What should an analyst look for to spot something untoward with regard to revenue recognition?

McConnell: As I mentioned, an analyst is never going to spot genuine fraud, such as booking sales to customers that don't exist. But basic fundamental analysis can help analysts identify revenue-recognition problems. Tracking "days-sales-in-receivables" and inventory turnover can reveal flaky accounting procedures as well as the fundamentals of a company's business operations. That said, lengthening days-sales-in-receivables does not necessarily mean that a company is booking sales before they should or that those sales do not exist, but it could mean that customers are paying more slowly or that the company is extending longer credit terms to their customers, neither of which is good. Such factors are indicative of the quality of the revenue and the business. Why do they have to extend longer credit terms? Why are their customers paying more slowly? Is the slower pay going to turn into an accounts receivable problem, or are customers going to return products? Such analysis helps detect not only fraud but also deterioration in the company's business.

Question: Will the FASB define the parameters of the estimates to be used in the fair value formula for employee stock options (i.e., volatility and the risk-free rate)?

---

[1] Bear, Stearns & Company, Inc., Equity Research, "Pension and Other Retirement Benefits I: A Historical Perspective" and "Pension and Other Retirement Benefits II: Forecasting 2002 Cost (Income)," *Accounting Issues* (November 2001). A copy of this report may be obtained by contacting Ms. McConnell at pmcconnell@bear.com.

McConnell: No, neither the FASB nor the IASB will mandate the parameters. If they did, those opposed to using the fair value method would argue that the numbers were not relevant because they were artificial and not applicable to a specific company. Because assumptions have to be company specific for the fair value method to work, analysts have to trust managements. Some guidance, such as saying that historic volatility is presumed to be the best indicator of future volatility, will be given (although it is a rebuttable presumption). In the past 18 months, managements in the United States have gotten a lot of egg on their faces. Nonetheless, the vast majority of corporate managements have integrity. Keep in mind that all numbers in financial statements are estimated. Every number a company records in its financial statement requires judgment, and most managements exercise their best judgment and adhere to high ethical standards. Unfortunately, all of corporate America seems to have been tainted by the bad behavior of a few financial executives.

Risk and Return Properties of Global Equities

Stefano F. Cavaglia
Head of Quantitative Strategies
UBS Global Asset Management (Americas) Inc.
Chicago

Vadim Moroz
Quantitative Analyst
UBS Global Asset Management (Americas) Inc.
Chicago

> Traditionally, global asset managers have focused primarily on country factors in selecting securities for a portfolio. But recent research indicates that this approach is no longer adequate because industry factors play a critical role in determining equity prices. Building on this new research, UBS Global Asset Management has developed a cross-industry, cross-country allocation framework for active equity portfolio managers to use when managing equity portfolios.

In the 20th century, global asset management relied heavily on a strategy that emphasized the country dimension in structuring international portfolio holdings. If an asset manager thought that Italy had good value, that manager bought equity positions in Italian companies. This strategy is no longer adequate. The global landscape has shifted, and the old paradigm does not take into account important changes in the way international businesses are structuring their operations now.

In this presentation, I will offer evidence about the global pricing of equities that demonstrates that the factor that really matters in global pricing is the industry of a business rather than its country of domicile. I will then propose an approach—one that we have developed at UBS Global Asset Management—that provides for a cross-industry, cross-country allocation for managing equity portfolios. Finally, I will discuss dynamic strategies for managing risks in this new paradigm.

The information I will present is based on research we have conducted at UBS, all of which has been published in the *Financial Analysts Journal*, *Journal of Investing*, and *Journal of Portfolio Management*.

Global Equity Management Paradigm of the 20th Century

Empirical evidence suggests that during the latter part of the 20th century, the predominant driver of global security prices was the country factor. That is, if an asset manager compared Fiat versus General Motors Corporation versus Toyota Motor Corporation, the key variable considered by the manager was the nationality of each of those businesses. Some of this inclination toward the country factor arose from the fact that asset managers had a tendency to build portfolios that were heavily biased in favor of their home countries. The reasons for creating these home-biased portfolios included high transaction costs, lack of familiarity with foreign markets, difficulty in obtaining information from outside the home country, and currency risk.

Besides home bias, much empirical evidence supported the tendency to choose equities based on country factors. For example, the correlation of returns

---

Editor's note: This material was presented at the conference by Dr. Cavaglia.

between equity and currency was close to zero and unstable; country exposure matched currency exposure. Thus, when asset managers thought about the exposure of a company such as Nestlé, their instinctive response would be, "Well, it is a Swiss company. It has 100 percent exposure to the Swiss franc." Further, such low correlation among markets lent a compelling justification for diversifying among countries, a justification reinforced by Solnik's 1974 *Financial Analysts Journal* article, which advised that diversifying across countries was an effective way of reducing risk.[1] Even more recent studies published in the *Financial Analysts Journal* seemed to substantiate the common wisdom. In 1989, Grinold, Rudd, and Stefek found evidence suggesting that country factors were more important than industry factors and were the critical determinants of the risk and return of a global portfolio.[2] In 1994 and 1999, Heston and Rouwenhorst arrived at similar conclusions by applying a somewhat different methodology.[3]

Looking back, one might ask whether the results were sensitive to the period analyzed, the data used, and the methodology applied. The last of these studies ended in 1998 and 1999, and global markets have changed since then. More important, the methodology in most of these studies slanted the results toward dominance of the country dimension over the industry dimension. And the cross-border equity data were so limited that in some instances, researchers were forced to use large granularities of industries. Indeed, in the 1994 study by Heston and Rouwenhorst, their consumer goods sector included funeral homes, software companies, pharmaceuticals, and car manufacturers—all clearly distinct economic activities. Thus, it should not be surprising to find that country factors dominate industry factors.

Nevertheless, these studies offered at the time the best evidence about the drivers of global equity prices. In light of this research and a prevailing home bias, most asset managers structured their portfolios around the country decision. Many established an easy-to-manage and highly accountable two-step allocation structure in which an equity strategy team charged with country selection was complemented by country directors charged with picking industries and stocks within countries. In this framework, the performance of each decision could be identified fairly accurately. If the equity strategists picked the wrong country, they were accountable. Similarly, country directors were accountable for the stocks they picked, and management could easily identify each director's ability to pick stocks within a country. Global portfolio data were arranged in a balance sheet (accounting style) that revealed the benchmark and the portfolio and active capitalization weights by country and currency. Each security was presumed to be 100 percent allocated to the country in which the company's headquarters was located or the country in which the company's stock was listed. Performance attribution systems, accounting systems, and risk systems were all oriented around the country dimension.

That was the paradigm of the last century. But times change; the world environment is dynamic, and managers are questioning whether this paradigm is still applicable.

Global Equity Management in the 21st Century

Several years ago, senior management at UBS started asking some basic questions about global markets and came to a number of conclusions.[4] The first conclusion was that the global economic environment had changed. Moreover, businesses were responding to this new environment, and their responses were leading to a change in the relative importance of the factors that drive security prices. In particular, the importance of country factors as a distinguishing characteristic of security prices was declining.

One indicator of this change is the convergence of interest rates. Interest rate differentials between country markets were substantial back in the late 1980s and early 1990s. With the convergence of economic policies and the formation of the EMU, however, one of the key distinguishing characteristics between countries—interest rates—has been removed.

Another indicator of the reduced importance of the country factor in equity returns is the growing significance of foreign sales, which now account for 40 percent of all global sales. Furthermore, consider that large- and mid-capitalization companies domiciled in Europe and Asia now account for 20 percent of U.S. domestic sales, which indicates that even the United States, which is often viewed as a monolith, is exposed to competitive pressure from non-U.S. companies.

---

[1] Bruno Solnik, "Why Not Diversify Internationally Rather Than Domestically?" *Financial Analysts Journal* (July/August 1974):48–54.

[2] Richard Grinold, Andrew Rudd, and Dan Stefek, "Global Factors: Fact or Fiction?" *Journal of Portfolio Management* (Fall 1989):79–88.

[3] Steven L. Heston and K. Geert Rouwenhorst, "Does Industrial Structure Explain the Benefits of International Diversification?" *Journal of Financial Economics* (June 1994):3–27 and K. Geert Rouwenhorst, "European Equity Markets and the EMU," *Financial Analysts Journal* (May/June 1999):57–64.

[4] Please see Gary P. Brinson, "Investment Management in the 21st Century," in *The Future of Investment Management* (Charlottesville, VA, 1998: AIMR):1–5.

Finally, consider how businesses have restructured their operations to focus on their core activities across borders. The best evidence of this restructuring can be found in cross-border mergers and acquisitions (M&As), which have risen dramatically over the past decade. If you look at the cross-border M&A activity of 10 years ago, such M&As were 50 percent intraindustry and 50 percent interindustry. Today, however, 70 percent of all cross-border M&As are intraindustry (e.g., banks buying other banks). Such a development suggests that businesses are focusing on their core activities while diversifying their operations globally. It also suggests that the industry dimension of equity performance may become more important than the country dimension.

Evidence of Global Equity Pricing

Jeff Diermeier, CIO of UBS, and Bruno Solnik (1974), an academic advisor for UBS, modeled the exposure of individual businesses to foreign factors. A good way to explain this model is through an example. Consider the case of Fiat. According to Diermeier and Solnik, Fiat is exposed to a country factor—Italy. It is also exposed to three regional factors—Europe, North America, and Asia. Further, Fiat is exposed to currency factors—the pound, yen, and U.S. dollar relative to the euro. To better understand the effect that each of these factors has on Fiat's share price, Diermeier and Solnik determined that each factor had to be isolated from the others. Thus, they purified the country factors affecting Fiat by removing the multinationals from the Italian index. Similarly, Diermeier and Solnik purified the regional factors by removing the relevant country factor—in this case, Italy. They were then able to statistically estimate the exposure of Fiat's share price to each of the factors—country, region, and currency. Diermeier and Solnik then documented that the sensitivity of a company's share price to foreign factors is closely related to the extent of its international activities.

This research is not merely a statistical exercise; the data indicate that the market is actually pricing the underlying fundamentals of the company. As another example, consider SmithKline Beecham, a U.K.-domiciled company with 92 percent of its sales generated outside of the United Kingdom.[5] The company's domestic beta is 0.17, and if the betas of the exposure of SmithKline Beecham to Asia, Europe (ex the United Kingdom), and North America are aggregated, the total is 0.94. The exposure to foreign currency factors is 0.46, which suggests that SmithKline Beecham is undertaking some form of currency hedging.

Now, consider an example relating to a national index—for example, that of Switzerland. The Swiss index is composed of Nestlé, UBS, Credit Suisse Group, and other companies domiciled in Switzerland. The assumption in the past was that a manager who established a Swiss market-capitalization-weighted portfolio would be buying an exposure to the Swiss domestic market. The statistical evidence shows, however, that while the manager would be buying an exposure of 0.45 to the Swiss market, he or she would be buying an even larger exposure of 0.60 to foreign markets—Asia, North America, and Europe (ex Switzerland).

Increasing Importance of Industry Factors. The evidence found by Diermeier and Solnik suggested that factors other than country of domicile—specifically regional and currency factors—were driving securities prices. In light of the observed global restructuring of companies, it appeared that global industry factors might be the source of these new valuation drivers. But quantitative evidence was needed to support this hypothesis, so Christopher Brightman, Michael Aked, and I conducted a study based on a universe of the equity securities of 5,000 companies to measure the relative importance of country and global industry factors.[6] We extracted the distinguishing country and industry characteristics from the historical time-series data of the prices of those 5,000 securities. Take Fiat as an example of one of these securities. From the historical data, we extracted the country factor (Italy) and the industry factor (autos), which allowed us to examine the effects of these two factors separately.

Our methodology followed that of Heston and Rouwenhorst (1994), who obtained country-factor returns from securities portfolios constructed to have the same industry composition. Thus, these country-factor returns can be thought of as country tilts that are industry neutral. Similarly, we obtained industry-factor returns from securities portfolios constructed to have the same country composition. These industry-factor returns can be thought of as industry tilts that are country neutral.

In this fashion, we obtain a time series of country returns (call them "pure country returns") and a time series of industry returns (call them "pure industry returns").

---

[5]SmithKline Beecham merged with Glaxo Wellcome on 27 December 2000 and is now called GlaxoSmithKline.

[6]Stefano Cavaglia, Christopher Brightman, and Michael Aked, "The Increasing Importance of Industry Factors," *Financial Analysts Journal* (September/October 2000):41–54.

Hypothetical Comparison. After extracting the country and industry factors from the historical data, we asked ourselves, "If an asset manager knew the industry and country returns ahead of time (i.e., had perfect foresight), which would produce the better portfolio return—a tilt toward the country factor or a tilt toward the industry factor?" To answer this question, we constructed two strategies based on perfect foresight. We assumed that each manager would create long–short portfolios proportional to capitalization weights. For example, if a country manager with perfect foresight knows that the U.S. equity market will rise, he or she will go long the United States in proportion to the market capitalization weight of the United States in the index. If the manager knows that Italy's equity market will fall, he or she will short Italy in proportion to the market capitalization weight of Italy in the index. The industry manager would follow the same strategy according to industry.

The weekly performance of the two managers—the country manager and the industry manager—from January 1987 to August 2002 is shown in **Figure 1**. The portfolios are based on the 22 developed equity markets that are constituents of the MSCI World Index through 31 May 2001. The y-axis indicates the percentage of return that exceeds the return of our world benchmark. In the first week of 1990, the industry manager earned a return of 0.4 percent above the benchmark and the country manager earned a return of 1.0 percent above the benchmark. The graph shows that, based on the parameters of our study, country tilts would have produced better returns in the early 1990s. In the more recent period beginning in the latter half of 1999, industry tilts would have produced better returns.

Figure 2 depicts the ratio of the performance of the industry manager to the country manager. Since the beginning of 1987, the industry effect has been twice as large as the country effect. An International Monetary Fund (IMF) study claims that if the technology sector is removed from this sort of analysis, the results shown in Figure 2 are not achieved.[7] But because the IMF study includes emerging markets that are excluded from our study, a comparison between the two is a bit misleading. Moreover, we have conducted our analysis on the universe of developed market equities (ex technology stocks) and have found that our general results are corroborated.

Diversifying Risk. Of course, returns are only one dimension of the equation. We must also consider risk. The well-known and generally accepted diagram of Bruno Solnik (1974), shown in Panel A of **Figure 3**, indicates that cross-country diversification was, at least at one time, more effective in reducing portfolio risk than was cross-industry diversification. But if we consider the past three years ending 30 August 2002, cross-industry diversification is more effective than cross-country diversification in reducing portfolio risk, as shown in Panel B of Figure 3. Further, diversifying across both country and industry is the best strategy. Both country and industry factors lower the overall risk, or volatility, of a portfolio.

---
[7] Robin Brooks and Marco del Negro, "The Rise in Comovement across National Stock Markets: Market Integration or Global Bubble?" Working Paper, International Monetary Fund (WP/02/147), 2002.

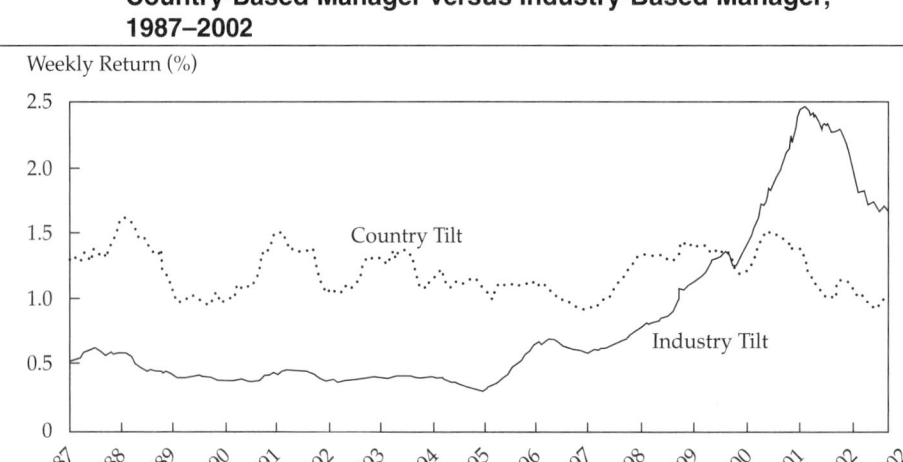

Figure 1. Performance of Alternative Perfect-Foresight Strategies: Country-Based Manager versus Industry-Based Manager, 1987–2002

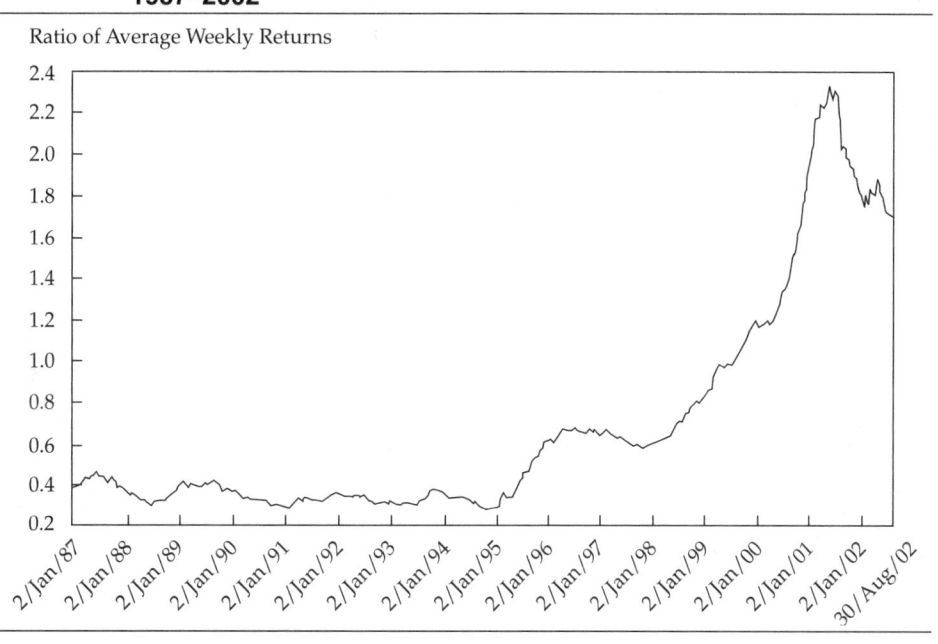

Figure 2. Relative Performance of Industry Tilts and Country Tilts, 1987–2002

Implications for Asset Management and Policymaking.
The lesson to be learned from this evidence is that asset managers can no longer ignore the foreign market activities of the companies in which they invest. Because the market now looks at underlying fundamentals to value companies, the conventional balance sheet approach to country and currency allocation—attributing a company to the country and currency of its headquarters' location—is problematic and biased. To make accurate country and currency allocations and thus assure adequate portfolio diversification, asset managers need to examine the underlying nature of a business.

Both the country and industry composition of a portfolio matter in quantifying the risk and return characteristics of a portfolio. Stock-selection opportunities may increasingly reside in relative comparisons of stocks within common global industries rather than within countries—for example, Fiat versus Toyota (intraindustry) rather than Fiat versus Alitalia (intracountry). Also, measures of risk need to be released from their provincial biases, and to do so, managers need to ask themselves how style factors, such as value, size, and momentum, are to be defined in this global environment. "Provincial" approaches to measuring style factors at a global level rely on an aggregation of the factors measured within countries; an alternative approach (that would be more consistent with recent empirical evidence) would rely on an aggregation of the factors measured within global industries. Further, analyst research teams should be reorganized to reflect a company's true competitive structure across geographical borders. Finally, portfolio construction should be based on a synthesis of top-down and bottom-up analysis.

The policy implications of these findings are especially important for plan sponsors. Home-biased portfolios are growing increasingly inefficient and result in unintended, active industry exposures. For example, a home-biased Swiss plan sponsor's portfolio is heavily tilted toward the banking and pharmaceuticals industries because these industries dominate the Swiss economy. The result is a poorly diversified portfolio on both the country and industry dimensions.

Allocation Matrix

To improve the effectiveness of asset allocation and thus the benefits of portfolio diversification under the new paradigm, we at UBS have developed a cross-industry/cross-country allocation framework—the CICCA matrix—which is discussed more fully in the November/December 2002 issue of the *Financial Analysts Journal*.[8]

Exhibit 1 illustrates the CICCA allocation matrix, which allows a manager to consider country and industry factors simultaneously. The top-down allocation decision should focus on industries within countries (local industries), which highlights the simultaneous importance of country and global industry factors. The matrix allocation process does not mandate a prescribed portfolio allocation to a

---
[8]Stefano Cavaglia and Vadim Moroz, "Cross-Industry, Cross-Country Allocation," *Financial Analysts Journal* (November/December 2002):78–97.

Figure 3. Cross-Country Diversification versus Cross-Industry Diversification

A. 3 January 1986–30 December 1994

Portfolio Variance (% of Average Stock Variance)

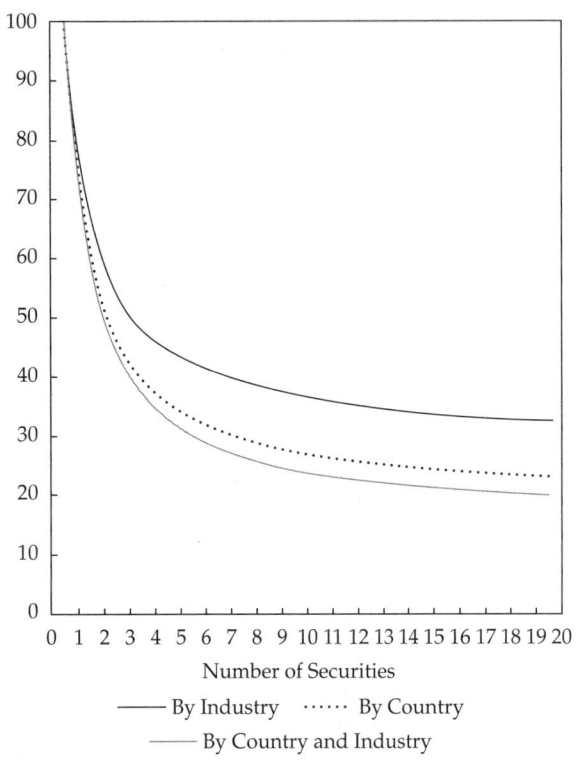

— By Industry ····· By Country
— By Country and Industry

B. Past Three Years Ending 30 August 2002

Portfolio Variance (% of Average Stock Variance)

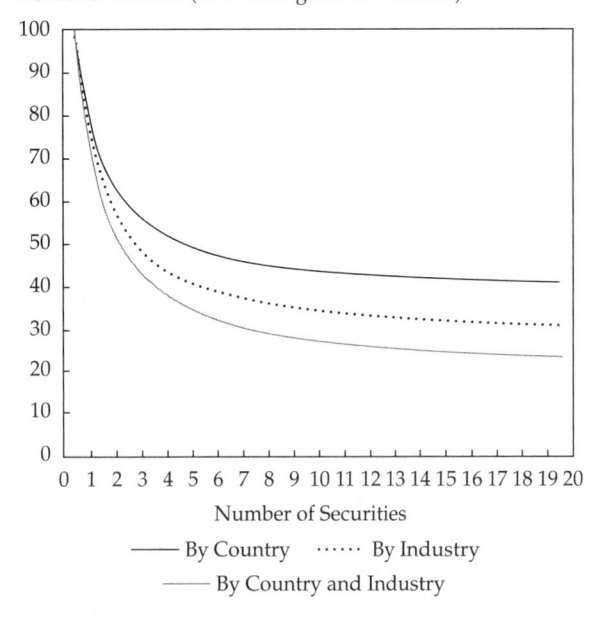

— By Country ····· By Industry
— By Country and Industry

Source: Based on data from the *Financial Times*, MSCI World Index, and UBS research.

country; rather, the CICCA allocations provide the first pass at the portfolio construction process in a country; therefore, a portfolio's allocation to Australia, for example, is none other than the sum of the positions in Australian industries. Similarly, global industry allocations will result from local industry decisions. Global style exposures, or style tilts, result from underlying local industry exposures; they are not decided at the aggregate level.

Exhibit 1. The CICCA Allocation Matrix

Australia	Austria	...	United Kingdom	United States
Energy				
Materials				
.				
.				
.				
Telecom services				
Utilities				

Once an asset manager has picked the local industries that present the greatest opportunities, he or she then selects stocks within each country/industry box. Security-selection decisions can be integrated with local industry exposures, and risk controls can be imposed that limit investment in one country or one global industry.

To make the CICCA framework practicable, we spent two years developing a proprietary database that encompasses the financial statements of companies in each of 23 national industries and 22 developed countries. The data start in 1985 and are continually updated to the present. Based on this information, we can develop forecasts that reflect a range of viewpoints.

Our approach can be illustrated with a simple analogy. In our everyday lives, when we are worried that it might rain, we perform a variety of tasks to determine if we should wear a raincoat. We listen to the weather report, we check to see if our neighbor is wearing a raincoat, and we look at the sky—three independent sources of information. We diversify our information signals so that if one of the signals is not accurate, the others might be.

For the CICCA framework, we use four forecast signals to predict the relative performance of local industries both in the short run and in the long run:

- momentum—excess total returns from the previous 12 months;
- value—dividend yield at time t and forward earnings yield estimate for the second fiscal year at time t;

- profitability—expected long-term earnings growth and the "up-down" ratio [(Upward earnings revisions minus downward earnings revisions)/Total estimate revisions at time t]; and a
- macroeconomic variable—yield of U.S. government long bond (10-year maturity at time t).

At any point in time, the combination of these signals can provide a return forecast for a local industry. For example, using these four signals, we can predict that the U.K. energy industry will outperform the global energy industry by 10 percent over the next three months. We can then attribute portions of the 10 percent outperformance estimate to specific sources, such as 3 percent from momentum, 2 percent from value, and 5 percent from profitability. Thus, the industry forecast is supported by explicit numbers that demonstrate relative performance. So, given any set of circumstances, we can forecast that one industry will outperform other industries by X percent, and we can attribute that X percent to various forecasting signals.

Asset managers can use these forecast signals in a variety of contexts. Three alternative models exist for applying the CICCA matrix approach to stock selection: the country-relative model, the industry-relative model, and the global-relative model. In the country-relative model, the manager emphasizes relative comparisons within countries. For example, a manager might look at a value signal, perhaps the dividend yield of companies in the U.K. energy industry relative to the dividend yield of all U.K. companies. The manager would then consider the dividend yield of the U.K. market relative to all other markets in the world. So, the attractiveness of one security is determined by a relative comparison within the country and then a comparison of the country to the rest of the world. Similarly, in the industry-relative model, a manager emphasizes relative company comparisons within global industries and chooses the companies with the strongest prospects for outperformance within each global industry. The global-relative model calls for relative comparisons on a full bottom-up basis (i.e., only the most attractive companies, regardless of country or industry, are chosen for investment). For each of these models, however, the same information is used; each merely structures the information in a different manner.

Applying CICCA to Historical Data

Before a manager would be willing to rely on this framework to manage a portfolio, he or she would want to test the functionality of the framework using historical data. The historical performance of the three models relative to the world benchmark for the period from 31 December 1990 to 30 June 2001 is presented in

Table 1. Constraints built into the models for this particular analysis include using a long-only strategy and applying overweights and underweights to particular securities, which constrains country exposures to ±10 percent, global industry exposures to ±10 percent, and national industry exposures to about 1 percent. As Table 1 shows, the gross average annualized return in excess of the world benchmark for the global-relative model was 400 bps; for the industry-relative model, 491 bps; and for the country-relative model, 426 bps. The industry-relative model had the best performance, but all three models are effective strategic tools. The *ex post* tracking errors for each model are relatively low. The historical information ratio is higher than 1, and the one-way turnover is about 50 percent. The turnover rate is sufficiently low that the alpha from the strategy would not be expected to be eliminated by real-world transaction costs. The risk-adjusted alpha incorporates a Jensen-like adjustment.[9] Perhaps the historical performance data reflects a (long-only) strategy that held high-beta stocks when the market was rising and low-beta stocks when the market was falling. In this case, the Jensen approach to calculate a risk-adjusted performance measurement would correct for the market effect.

Table 1. Historical Performance of Global-, Industry-, and Country-Relative Models in Excess of the World Benchmark, 31 December 1990–30 June 2001

Historical Performance	Global-Relative Model	Industry-Relative Model	Country-Relative Model
Gross average annualized return in excess of benchmark	4.00%	4.91%	4.26%
Ex post annualized tracking error	2.87%	3.48%	2.85%
Information ratio	1.22	1.26	1.32
Turnover	50.40%	54.30%	49.00%
Best annual performance	9.96%	13.18%	10.81%
Worst annual performance	–2.98%	–1.86%	–3.28%
Risk-adjusted alpha	3.30%	4.52%	3.62%

In addition to systematic exposures to market risk, we consider other risk factors—value, size, and momentum. Measuring these risks in a global context requires some care. The value style factor is measured

[9] Jensen's measure, or alpha, can be used to help determine if a portfolio is earning the correct return for its level of risk. Jensen's measure is calculated as $\alpha_p = \bar{r}_p - [\bar{r}_f + \beta_p(\bar{r}_m - \bar{r}_f)]$. For more, please see Michael C. Jensen, "Risk, the Pricing of Capital Assets, and the Evaluation of Investment Portfolios," *Journal of Business* (April 1969):167–247.

with a self-financing portfolio that is long stocks with a high dividend yield and short stocks with a low dividend yield; "size" factor returns are obtained by being long large-capitalization stocks and short low-capitalization stocks; and "momentum" factor returns are obtained by being long stocks with high returns for the previous 12 months and short stocks with low returns over the same period. For each risk factor that we consider, we compute three alternative data sorts. The country-relative sort obtains the global risk factor from an aggregation of the country factors; the industry-relative sort obtains the global risk factor from an aggregation of the industry factors; and the global-relative sort obtains the global risk factor from an aggregation that ignores both the country and industry association of a particular company.[10] The historical performance of the capitalization-weighted factors for the period 31 December 1985 to 30 June 2001 is presented in **Table 2**. Clearly, how one sorts the data (or rather, which relative comparison one makes) can significantly affect the risk premium that is estimated.

The Jensen-like correction that we apply to our returns in excess of the benchmark considers all possible combinations of risk factors (computed with the sorts we have identified). We report all possible risk-adjusted alphas in our recent *Financial Analysts Journal* articles, and for the purpose of exposition, we report the median risk-adjusted alpha in Table 1. In all cases, we find that our alphas are economically large and statistically significant. Further, we find that the industry-relative forecast model outperforms the country-relative forecast model in all cases, suggesting that relative comparisons within industries provide a more effective means of adding value, as compared with relative comparisons within countries.

---

[10] For a more detailed explanation of these sorting techniques, please see Cavaglia and Moroz (2002).

Table 2. Capitalization-Weighted Annualized Monthly Returns by Style for Global-, Industry-, and Country-Relative Models, 31 December 1985–30 June 2001

Style	Global-Relative Model	Industry-Relative Model	Country-Relative Model
Value	1.84	4.29	2.73
Size	–5.23	–1.06	–0.29
Momentum	9.29	3.10	3.00

Note: Value = long stocks with high dividend yield, short stocks with low dividend yield; size = long large-capitalization stocks, short low-capitalization stocks; momentum = long stocks with high 12-month past returns, short stocks with low past returns.

This analysis suggests that an alpha (not yet identified) exists that is in excess of the risk factors that we identified (Cavaglia and Moroz 2002). No matter which model is used—country relative or industry relative—an alpha that cannot be explained by the risk factors is found. So, where is this alpha coming from? Perhaps at some point, someone will identify a risk factor that will explain this source of the alpha.

Conclusion

Globalization has spurred a change in the factors that determine securities pricing. The CICCA approach developed at UBS provides a framework for managing equity portfolios based on this change. CICCA provides dynamic forecasts that are most effective within and across industries. These forecasts are obtained from a blend of style signals, and they can be used to produce significant returns in excess of the world benchmark. The "anomaly" we document presents interesting challenges and opportunities for the investment and academic communities.

Question and Answer Session

Stefano F. Cavaglia

Question: Industry effects seem to have been stronger when the market was strong. Why should that be, and is this tendency unrelated to the bull market/bear market issue?

Cavaglia: I do not know, but it seems intuitively clear that both country and industry effects will be drivers of fundamentals, and thus stock prices, regardless of the direction of the market. You seem to be asking, "Should I bet on industries in up markets and countries in down markets?" An alternative and related question is: "If I cannot bet on industries in up markets or countries in down markets, will CICCA still outperform?" In this case, I do know. Our backtests suggest that CICCA will still outperform.

Question: What practical advice do you have for all those whose mandates are constrained by country?

Cavaglia: Our firm has made a strong and intellectually sound statement to its clients: Go global. The reality of transitioning from country and regional mandates to global mandates is challenging, and we are working with our clients to facilitate the transition process. We have been working on this transition for years in our fundamental investment portfolios. We also introduced a more quantitative global hedge fund. About a year ago, we spoke to some of the European pension plans, who told us, "Yes, we believe in your concept. Our universities are teaching the findings of your research in graduate business schools. But the reality is that our business, as plan sponsors, is structured on a regional basis. How can you, UBS, help us in the transition from country mandates to global mandates?" Our response was to establish a long–short global fund and let the plan sponsor use it in the alternative investment space. Once the plan sponsor has it in that space, the plan's managers can start the dialogue with their board members on transitioning to global investment. The transition is not going to happen overnight, but one effective way of getting boards to consider the concept of global investing is to start an intense, performance-driven dialogue on this issue.

Question: You seem to rely heavily on quantitative methods. Where do fundamentals fit in?

Cavaglia: The long–short portfolio discussed here primarily uses quantitative methods, although with a fundamental assist. In our mainline portfolios, we are fundamentally driven with quantitative support. To address the fundamentals, our analysis is structured on a global industry basis, so that when we construct a global energy portfolio, our analysts choose the stocks they like globally for the energy sector. Then, a portfolio construction team takes those inputs and builds a global portfolio, regional portfolio, world-minus-the-U.S. portfolio, and so on. The portfolio construction at UBS starts with our analysts picking stocks on an industry-relative basis. In the next step of the process, the portfolio construction team uses the industry-relative information to build global portfolios. The quantitative analysts (of which I am one) use fundamental data as inputs in a model-driven framework that is more statistical (rather than judgmental) in nature. This model-driven framework is used to create a return forecast and a resulting trade. The fundamental and quantitative approaches are complementary, and the two together can lead to superior risk-adjusted performance.

Adapting Fundamental Analysis for Cross-Border Valuation

Sophie Blanpain
Head of Equity Research
Morley Fund Management
London

> Although fundamental principles of valuation apply to cross-border analysis, analysts must adjust for differences in accounting and local business practices. Pure financial analysis can be misleading, and failure to understand the local context of a company's operations can result in serious valuation errors. P/E ratios are easily distorted in cross-border analysis, but with certain adjustments, P/E can be a valuable analytical tool.

I believe that we in the investment management industry have a tendency to overemphasize accounting differences (whether on a cross-border or interindustry basis) and downplay differences in business practices. For example, consider the value judgments that U.S. or U.K. investors make about the way that companies in continental Europe operate, and vice versa. The business practices followed in particular countries or regions were adopted for good reasons and are expected to be optimal within their local context. Thus, to escape becoming mired in accounting incomparables and questionable value judgments, I recommend that when performing cross-border and interindustry analysis, analysts return to analytical basics and take advantage of the concept of real P/E.

Major Accounting Differences

The four accounting and financial reporting areas responsible for the majority of differences are pensions, goodwill, provisions, and depreciation. For analysts who rely on ratio analysis, the accounting differences within each of these areas can significantly distort comparative ratios, and analysts need to adjust for these differences as part of their analytical procedure. Although the harmonization of global accounting standards is under way, accounting and reporting differences are likely to persist for the foreseeable future and must be integrated into comparative company analysis.

Consider a real, if extreme, example of the distortions of earnings per share that can arise from different accounting standards. DaimlerChrysler was first listed on the NYSE in 1993, which was a bad year for German companies. In fact, the German stock market reported a loss that year. In the first nine months of 1993, under German accounting standards, Daimler reported a loss of $100 million. Prior to listing on the NYSE, under U.S. GAAP, Daimler reported that the restated loss for the same nine-month period was more than $1.0 billion. This huge difference in reported earnings was largely attributable to the elimination (under U.S. GAAP) of the positive impact of accounting provisions commonly used by German companies to smooth earnings. This dramatic shift in reported earnings under different accounting systems highlights the importance of questioning the reported numbers and delving into the underlying precepts that support the numbers.

The first step in a valuation analysis is adjusting for the differences among countries' accounting standards. An analyst typically will reconcile to the accounting standards of the country in which most of the assets he or she is involved with are located. For those who require assistance in making these adjustments, many sell-side companies publish informative guides about how to reconcile one standard with another.

The next step in valuation analysis goes beyond adjusting for accounting differences and involves understanding how a company's business practices can influence the way it operates. Most ratio analysis is flawed because it tends to include only the accounting side of the equation and ignores business practices. In the recent past, the constant focus on the income statement and reported earnings has diverted attention from the balance sheet. The faulty valuations that have run roughshod through the investment management industry lately are partly the fault of buy-side analysts. If we had made our forecasts based on balance sheets, as well as income statements, and required that sell-side analysts do the same, we could have escaped relatively unscathed.

Business Practices

As I mentioned previously, cross-border valuation challenges often stem from a lack of knowledge about the ways in which companies in different countries operate. Knowledge of local business practices is a necessary tool for analysts charged with the valuation of companies operating in countries and regions other than their own. The following examples highlight how differences in business practices can influence the most commonly used financial ratios and other valuation methodologies.

Ownership versus Leasing of Assets. Leasing assets, instead of owning them, can have a dramatic effect on the comparative analysis of companies. A good illustration of this point is the way in which U.K. and French food retailers operate in their respective countries. According to French accounting standards, French companies can lease assets without having to record them on their balance sheets. A recent U.K. inquiry to determine whether U.K. consumers were being ripped off by U.K. food retailers was partially attributable to this French accounting standard and its impact on the operating margins of French food retailers. One reason given for the investigation was that the net margin of U.K. retailers was about twice that of French retailers, if not slightly higher. The net-margin argument, however, ignored the difference between the accounting standards in the two countries. Because French companies are allowed to keep leased assets off the balance sheet, they typically choose not to own the land and buildings from which they operate; instead, they tend to enter into long-term leases (generally 10 years). French food retailers thus make annual lease payments that are shown as a line item on their income statements, whereas U.K. food retailers, which usually own both the land and the buildings in which they operate, do not have similar lease costs on their income statements.

Clearly, analysts who scrutinized only the readily apparent differences in the financial statements of the two countries' food retailers missed the point. Food retailers do not make any more of a profit in the United Kingdom than they do in France. The companies merely account for their operations differently, and the difference relates to the leasing of assets. Considering the fact that land typically does not depreciate and buildings depreciate over much longer terms than do leases, French companies can have enormous annual leasing charges that U.K. companies do not have. Although U.K. companies do have depreciation charges, the charges are much lower than the French companies' leasing charges. The equalizing factor between the two is the significant capital required by U.K. companies for the purchase of their land and property. The actual invested capital of both countries' retailers is approximately the same. In fact, the differential in the cost of capital between the two countries is only about 1.5 percent, so the excess return generated by the U.K. and French food retailers on their respective invested capital, or the value creation of the two countries' retailers, is not significantly different. Nevertheless, relying solely on the reported numbers would have misled analysts in their comparative analysis of U.K. and French retailers.

Working Capital Requirements. A second business practice that can affect the comparability of financial statements is the working capital requirement. For example, the payment term for purchased merchandise in the United Kingdom is 30 days, and most customers will pay at, or by, 30 days. In France, however, the payment term is closer to 90 days. The result is that the amount of capital needed to run a business is much lower in France than it is to run the same business in the United Kingdom. When a French retailer opens a store, the retailer basically has a net-cash inflow. The building in which the business operates is leased and does not require invested capital. The retailer's working capital is effectively being financed because the payment term for purchased goods is so long. By the time the retailer has to pay for goods sold, the goods have actually been sold and the cash is available to make the payment. Thus, the overall invested capital of French retailers tends to be low compared with that of their U.K. counterparts.

Relationships with Suppliers and Customers. Another important business practice distinction is a company's relationship with its suppliers and customers. Companies often negotiate different terms with suppliers and customers based on their cash flow position. Anytime an analyst observes a difference in the margin behavior of two companies in the same business or industry, he or she should always be alert to the games that companies play with suppliers and customers in order to boost margins.

For example, if a company has a strong cash position, it may offer interest-free credit to customers, which creates the appearance of improving margins because the company can more easily raise the price of its goods. To avoid missing this trick, analysts have to evaluate not only the income statement but also the relationship between the income statement and the balance sheet. Having a fully integrated valuation model that can forecast the income statement, working capital, and the complete balance sheet is absolutely essential. The beauty of such a model is that, even though the profit-and-loss section of the model will be detailed, the rest of the model will be relatively simple and straightforward. It can help analysts understand that companies with dissimilar income statements differ simply because their business practices differ.

Implications for Ratio Analysis. Ratio analysis is useful if analysts adjust their ratios for accounting differences such as those mentioned previously, but these adjustments are extremely time consuming. Going back to my earlier example of food retailers, in 1997, we at Morley Fund Management noticed that the P/Es for U.S., U.K., and French retailers appeared to be extremely different, which was a bit strange. After all, the retail industry is not a high-growth industry and is fairly stable; real options models are hardly necessary to analyze it.

We found that as we moved up the income statement from earnings, or away from an analysis based on P/E, to an analysis based on earnings before interest and taxes (EBIT), for which the numbers become more stable, the cross-border relationships appeared to be closer. We concluded that for cross-border valuations, enterprise value (EV)/EBIT will typically be a better basis of comparison than P/E. At the time of our analysis, EV/EBIT for U.K., U.S., and French retailers ranged from 10 to 15, quite a wide range but narrower than the range of P/Es for the same companies. French retailers are not at the high end of the EV/EBIT range because their EBITs are depressed by extremely high leasing costs.

When we moved further up the income statement to an analysis based on sales, we found the range of EV/sales was much narrower than that of EV/EBIT. In other words, per dollar sold, the overall profitability of U.K., U.S., and French retailers was similar, so the ratio of EV/sales was sending a signal to alert shareholders that those companies had a similar level of profitability at the time of the analysis.

Forget about ratios that are driven purely by reported earnings; the ratios derived from further up the income statement are better comparative measures for cross-border valuation analysis. And unless the companies being compared have a similar profit structure and the industry is truly international, ratio analysis is useless. Of course, that is not such bad news because hardly anyone uses ratio analysis for long-term valuations anyway.

Salvaging P/E for Cross-Border Valuation

P/E, which was one of the first valuation concepts and one of the first ratios used in comparative company analysis, remains extremely popular. P/E ratios are easily distorted, but the underlying concept is solid. One problem analysts must be aware of, however, is that accounting P/Es can differ from real P/Es.

Weaknesses. P/Es are flawed for cross-border valuations (and in absolute terms) for five reasons. Accounting differences are the most obvious problem. For example, if a German company makes a DM1 billion provision, that provision is not translatable under another country's accounting standards. A second problem is the lack of comparability of invested capital because of differences in depreciation. A third problem is cost of capital, and a fourth problem is that P/E is a static measure and does not account for a company's growth prospects.

But the most critical problem for cross-border valuation is that P/E fails to adjust for economic cycles. Analysts have to make sure that the companies being compared are at exactly the same point in the cycle; otherwise, they should forget about using P/E altogether. Essentially, however, P/E can be a valuable analytical tool—with adjustments. P/E equals P/book value (BV), which is a valuation measure, divided by E/BV, or the return on equity (ROE). Thus, P/E equals P/BV divided by ROE.

Figure 1 illustrates the fundamental concept behind P/E: The price an investor is willing to pay for an equity (i.e., P/BV) is a function of how much that equity returns (i.e., ROE). In most of the countries we have analyzed, however, the R^2, or the line of best fit, is approximately 10 percent or less, demonstrating that the correlation between the two factors is weak. But adjusting P/BV and ROE for distortions caused by such items as financial leverage and capital employed (CE) increases the R^2 to about 25 percent. As shown in **Exhibit 1**, the pure accounting-based

Exhibit 1. Adjusting for Financial Leverage and CE Distortions

P/BV → EV/CE → EV/IC
ROE → ROCE → ROIC

Figure 1. Correlation between Price Paid and Return Generated

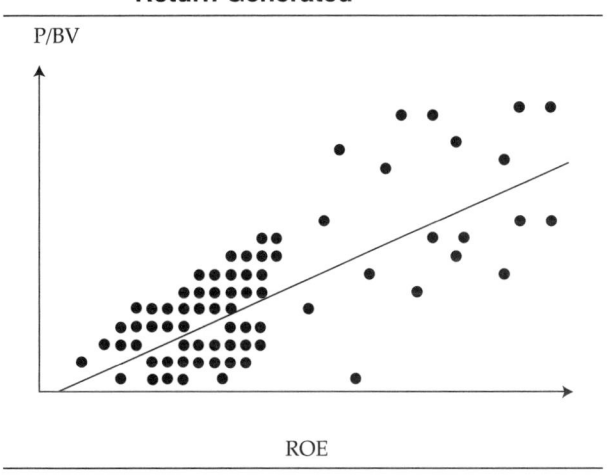

Note: Dots represent generic assets.

P/BV and ROE can be adjusted to arrive at more realistic measures of invested capital (IC), which can definitely improve the relationship between price and expected return.

Adjustments. The main adjustments to CE, and thus to traditional P/E, should be made for the following items:
- written-off assets (should be added back),
- depreciation (should be economic, not accounting),
- goodwill (should be added back and, if necessary, amortized),
- leasing (should be capitalized),
- inflation (should be current, not historic, cost accounting, where possible), and
- R&D and advertising expenses (should be capitalized).

To illustrate the importance of adding back assets that have been written off, imagine that three years ago, at the height of the tech bubble, you invested most of your clients' assets in technology stocks. And suppose that the stocks' value decreased by 50 percent when the tech bubble burst. If you asked your clients if you could calculate their portfolios' total return based on 50 percent of the assets they gave you to manage (the current value after writing off the loss in value), those clients would not be happy. The likelihood of your clients saying "no problem" is small, yet corporations are permitted to write off assets without any explanation. If analysts do not adjust for these write-offs, their analyses will be faulty.

Figure 2 shows the "valuation matrix" for the S&P 500 Index, which is really Figure 1 adjusted (as I have just described) to a real P/E. We back tested the matrix in the United States and found a cross-sectional relationship with an R^2 of about 70 percent, so this approach provides a stronger link between a company's value (defined as EV/IC) and return on invested capital (defined as ROIC) and is reasonably easy to calculate. The pivot point of this slope is the cost of capital. It is the point of perfect neutrality, at which the investor would be willing to pay a multiple of one times assets if the ROIC was exactly equal to the cost of capital. The steeper the slope, the more one unit of ROIC costs. We back tested this relationship and found that the slope in the valuation matrix explains the historical pattern of growth as it is priced by the market. In **Figure 3**, we have plotted the actual

Figure 2. Valuation Matrix for S&P 500 Companies, Third Quarter 1999

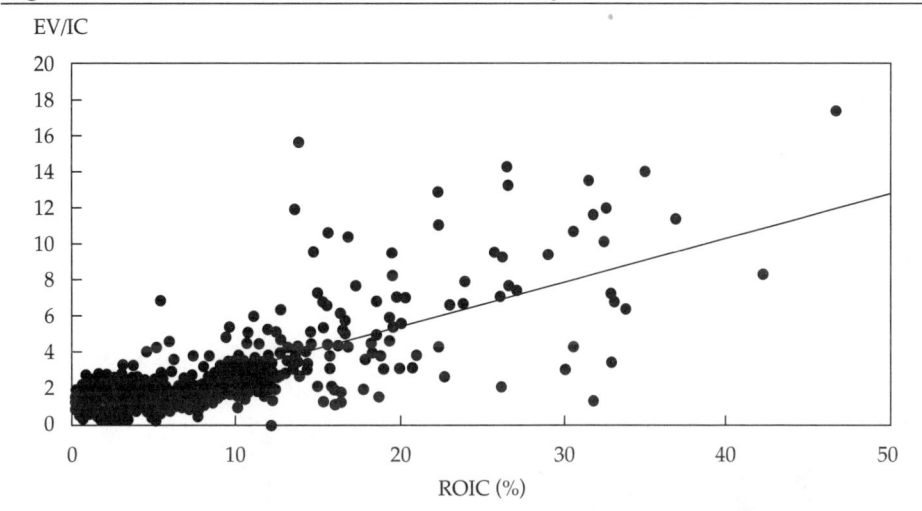

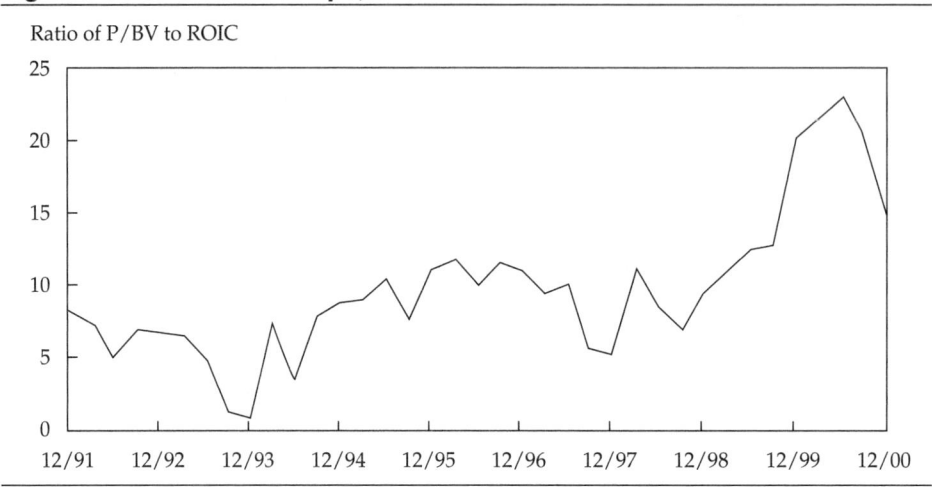

Figure 3. The Matrix's Slope, December 1991–December 2000

slope of the line of best fit for the past 10 years. One of the most stable measures of long-term performance is the ability of companies to improve on ROIC, the main driver of a company's performance. A company can grow fast, but if it does so unprofitably, it will merely lose money. The valuation matrix is most accurate within a single country, but it can be used on a cross-country basis when adjustments are made for the major accounting differences among countries.

Conclusion

The fundamental principles of valuation clearly apply to cross-border businesses and assets, but differences in accounting and, more important, local business practices must be recognized. Analysts should strive to understand the local context that drives a company's operations and should recognize that no amount of financial analysis can substitute for good judgment in this process.

After the cross-border and interindustry adjustments are made to enhance comparability, analysts need to construct a full-fledged discounted cash flow model, which is the valuation procedure followed by most analysts. Moreover, analysts need to follow a top-down approach in valuing a company. Whatever model is used must be calibrated to take into account the fundamental equation Growth = ROIC × Reinvestment. The only way a company can grow is by reinvesting some of the cash it generates through its ROIC. Analysts then must decide whether the company can generate returns above its cost of capital and whether the company can grow faster than the economy. Getting bogged down in the accounting minutiae can distract analysts from this fundamental concept.

A Pragmatic Approach to Cross-Border Valuation

Gerco Goote
Senior Vice President and Global Coordinator of Equity Research
ABN AMRO Asset Management
Amsterdam

> Cross-border comparability of companies is complicated not only by accounting differences but also by country- and industry-specific business practices. The key is to build a solid qualitative understanding of a company as a foundation for quantitative analysis; otherwise, the quantitative findings will be unreliable. ABN AMRO Asset Management has found that consistent value creation is a critical factor in long-term performance, and thus, it uses an approach in which cash flow return on investment is a critical valuation parameter.

As capital markets become more global and companies and investors increasingly venture beyond their domestic borders, analysts must grapple with the challenge of widely varying accounting standards among countries. In theory, global accounting standards should facilitate apples-to-apples comparisons in cross-border valuation and stock selection, but in practice, issues other than accounting may frustrate comparability. The entrenchment of country-specific business practices suggests that the adoption of global accounting standards will not be able to fully address all cross-border valuation inconsistencies.

At ABN AMRO Asset Management, we see ourselves as pioneers in global industry investment and analysis. In the mid-1980s, when we first undertook cross-border valuation analysis, data were unreliable and accounting systems were even more diverse than they are now. Thus, our analytical approach was a pragmatic one, largely qualitative. As data became more available and reliable by the end of the 1990s, however, we increasingly incorporated quantitative tools into our work. Today, the combination of both qualitative and quantitative approaches in cross-border valuation has proven to be successful.

Major Challenges

The most significant cross-border valuation challenges stem from three areas: comparability of accounts (i.e., differences in accounting standards), business practice assessments (i.e., translating business plans into data that can be compared), and analysis of global competitive structures (i.e., the appetite for products made or services rendered).

Cross-border valuation inevitably entails a great deal of interpretation to obtain reliable numbers. As an econometrician, I tend not to take any number at face value. Analysts should analyze carefully the numbers they use to evaluate a company and be sure to understand them completely before basing decisions on them.

Comparability of Accounts. Accounting creates more noise than insight. Accountants perpetually restate the past in order to be right at a certain moment in time, as is evident from the frequent restatements of company accounts. Analysts have to understand that a financial statement is essentially a restatement document, not a truly straightforward depiction of the past period's performance; in fact, it represents a successive series of restatements from previous periods. Also, because accountants tend to think about the present, not the future, they focus on a short time horizon.

Another problem is that accountants tend to place more importance on taxes than on shareholder value. To arrive at the lowest tax liability for a company, accountants have no choice but to follow the accounting rules of the country in which the company is located. As a result, the reported financial information of these companies is not comparable.

In addition, competitive pressures among companies can lead to questionable assumptions and restatements designed to enhance the reported financial position of a company. Accounting irregularities arise from the subjectivity involved in the estimation process that is used to present the most favorable numbers possible to investors.

To sidestep these accounting issues, at ABN AMRO, our solution is to restate all items back to cash and then apply the same accounting schemes for all similar companies and assume the same discount rates for all similar companies. At the end of the day, the cash inflows and outflows for a company matter most.

Because of the short-term goals and subjective element in accounting, global accounting standards are not a solution to cross-border valuation challenges. Global accounting standards are, after all, subject to the interpretation of individual accountants. The wide spectrum of the possible interpretations of accounting standards makes the task of translating all accounting transactions to cash a worthwhile endeavor.

Business Practice Assessments. Before starting a company valuation, analysts first have to understand how a company operates. Diving into the numbers alone will not provide sufficient knowledge of why a company operates as it does. Danger lies in believing you understand the numbers before obtaining the relevant qualitative information through which to filter them. An incomplete analysis can lead to a premature opinion (positive or negative) on the value of a company.

At ABN AMRO, we try to understand the qualitative factors first, before digging into the quantitative data. We strongly believe in applying a balanced research process that incorporates understanding the global industry, with all its complexities and competitive structures, as well as the company's business practices. We particularly want to pinpoint whether a company is merely lucky or actually highly skilled at what it does on a day-to-day basis. Many companies are simply lucky.

Global Competitive Structure Analysis. Once we make an assessment of a company's business practices, we then turn to a global growth assessment and valuation to justify our view of the company. We do not start with the numbers and work backwards to justify our business practice assessment.

We take a global scenario approach. At ABN AMRO, we look for companies that create value in excess of their cost of capital. How much value a company is creating and the fact that it is growing its business are characteristics that can be compared—on a global basis—with the performance of other companies. We can evaluate how wisely a company makes capital expenditure and reinvestment decisions and determine the opportunities and challenges such a company is likely to find in the future.

We also compare a company with its industry peers. Global comparability is likely to exist within industries because many industries have developed a global competitive structure. We are careful to compare a company versus its peers in different time periods. Because we use a discounted cash flow (DCF) model, understanding the financial accounts being compared and the business practices of the companies being compared is crucial before a final valuation decision can be made.

To tackle cross-border accounting differences, we adhere to the motto "cash is king." With cash as our basis of comparison, our final step in valuation is to apply a global discount rate for comparability in a DCF model. This last step, however, is not the most important. Many more numbers have to be compared before constructing a final DCF model. An obsession with the need to reach a final number, whether a final share price or a final project value, can generate a hastily and incorrectly estimated discount rate and cash flows that are overstated or understated for the periods in the analysis. Instead of focusing on the derivation of a single number, a thorough period-by-period analysis, which encompasses many data points, will provide a much better valuation tool than the output of a DCF model, which is a single data point. As we all know, the share price is an indicator of the cash flow that the company is expected to generate in the future. Our analysis reveals that the discounted long-term growth prospects of a company often are not reflected in the share price.

Value Creation

ABN AMRO conducted a study with CSFB HOLT that confirmed that consistent value creation creates long-term outperformance. HOLT's platform is the key to our internal valuation analysis. We have confidence in HOLT's historical database, in which many items have been restated back to cash using a methodology for which we have a high comfort level. We create the future scenarios we wish to test within the valuation system based on I/B/E/S International's return estimates and our own return estimates.

Table 1 shows the range of cash flow return on investment (CFROI) for seven years (historical return for the past five years plus two years of forecast returns as of September 2002). The companies that have shown stable CFROIs over those seven years are divided into four CFROI ranges. Each company in the

Table 1. Value Creation over Weighted-Average Cost of Capital

Average MSCI World Index CFROI Cuts[a]	CFROI FY (–4)	CFROI FY (–3)	CFROI FY (–2)	CFROI FY (–1)	CFROI FY0	CFROI FY1	CFROI FY2	5-Year Total Shareholder Return
0–5%	2.49	2.32	2.62	3.04	2.69	2.86	3.31	–5.29%
5–10%	7.25	7.24	7.22	7.37	7.34	7.1	7.31	23.19
10–15%	12.2	12.15	12.94	12.44	12.15	12.31	12.28	53.26
>15%	24.63	25.54	25.04	24.43	24.76	22.84	21.99	72.82

FY = fiscal year; FY0 ends September 2002.

[a]Screened companies that meet the CFROI criteria for the past five years and forecasted for the next two years.

Source: Based on data from CSFB Holt.

---

study maintained the same profile each year; the companies are not mixed from one group to another. These groups of companies are taken from the MSCI World Index, and each of the four groups contains at least 40 companies.

Table 1 shows that total shareholder return for the past five years would have been excellent (72.82 percent, on average) if only the foresight of knowing which companies would earn seven years of stable CFROIs above 15 percent had been possible. Of course, that degree of foresight is the Holy Grail of investing, but an analyst can seriously improve his or her valuation ability by thinking in terms of predicting a series of CFROIs instead of a single value from a DCF model. The companies with the best performance are the ones that actually move from the 0–5 percent CFROI range toward the greater than 15 percent CFROI range. We seek those companies that are able to significantly improve their CFROIs over time (such as Ryanair, Porsche, Nissan Motor Company, Sony Corporation, and BMW AG). If you can identify companies that you believe will be able to dramatically raise their CFROI, complex DCF models are not needed. These types of companies, whether they are in Europe, the United States, or Asia, are riding a wave of excellent returns. As our research shows, companies with high CFROIs are able to maintain those returns over a period of five years and longer.

Key Questions

Analysts have to make their comparisons of companies as pure as possible by avoiding valuations that rely merely on heaps of numbers. Differences in accounting standards mean that analysts have to develop a sound knowledge of the global industry and combine that knowledge with an accurate business practice assessment before plugging in the numbers. Answering the following questions will help focus this process and lead to a more accurate valuation:

- Do I understand the drivers of this global industry? Do I really understand where the money is being made?
- Do I understand the companies that are active in this global industry?
- Do I understand the long-term objectives of the companies? Analysts tend to focus on next year, but they should look further ahead. Is the company muddling through, simply doing what it has done for ages, or is it thinking about the changes in the world that could cause it to alter its way of doing things?
- Do I understand the value creation proposition?
- Do I understand what the weighted-average cost of capital (WACC) means for a company and the return the company needs to earn in excess of its WACC?
- Can I estimate the rate over the next five years of growth and return for the company? Answering that question helps an analyst understand the market's implied five-year growth assumptions for the company, which is where valuation begins—comparing the string of implied growth rates, which are already factored into the share price, with the string of an analyst's own estimates for growth.
- Do I understand how the company compares with its peers? This question can be answered by judging the relative value of a company versus its peers based on the comparison of a string of variables estimating growth and return for the company against the same string of variables for its peers.

Conclusion

Successful cross-border valuation is possible if analysts begin with a starting point of cash (which means restating accounting transactions back to cash) and adopt a pragmatic (qualitative) approach. A solid understanding of business practices should underlie the quantitative analysis that complements the qualitative approach; otherwise, quantitative analysis is a useless endeavor. Cross-border valuation should begin before the final parameter is found (e.g., the single value from a DCF model) but should begin on the inputs to that parameter, such as the series of periodic growth and return assumptions that drive the CFROI of the company. In addition, to obtain accurate results in a global valuation environment, an analyst must choose the right company factors to compare. CFROI is a good tool if the analyst's views on a company can be translated into the different scenarios that underlie the estimated cash flows. In short, analysts have to do the work themselves. There is no Holy Grail. No single system will provide all the answers, but if analysts begin at the right starting point (cash flows), their valuation abilities will be much improved.

Reconciling the Numbers from Multiple GAAPs

Pieter Dekker
Senior Manager
Ernst & Young LLP
London

> Differences in accounting standards among the United States, United Kingdom, and countries of continental Europe complicate cross-border valuations. Analysts should pay attention to seven areas in particular: business combinations and goodwill, consolidation and special purpose entities, leasing, pension accounting, deferred taxation, share-based payments (employee stock options), and revenue recognition. A firm understanding of accounting treatments in these seven areas will enable analysts to perform more meaningful comparative company analysis.

Part of my job responsibilities at Ernst & Young in London is to answer colleagues' questions from all around Europe on how to apply International Accounting Standards (IAS). As a result, I have learned a lot about accounting practices in Europe, and what I have learned is that they are often horrendous. In the context of such practices, this presentation is intended to enlighten analysts on critical differences among IAS, U.K. generally accepted accounting practices (GAAP), U.S. generally accepted accounting principles (GAAP), and various European GAAP frameworks.

GAAP

What is GAAP anyway? Should analysts care about differences in GAAP from country to country? This section is a guided tour of a number of GAAP differences that are important or tend to give rise to major accounting difficulties.

What Is GAAP? The term "generally accepted accounting principles" raises a few questions. The first question is: accepted where? Typically, the principles in question are accepted in only one country (and sometimes within only a particular industry), and thus we have U.S. GAAP, U.K. GAAP, Dutch GAAP, and so forth. These various GAAP frameworks differ in surprising ways.

The second question is: accepted by whom? Typically, auditors or the accounting industry draft accounting standards, with some input from preparers and users of accounts, but mainly, accounting standards are prepared by accountants for other accountants. Consequently, accounting standards do not necessarily take into account the information needs of other parties, such as investment analysts.

Even the acronym GAAP can mean different things. In the United States, GAAP means generally accepted accounting *principles*. In the United Kingdom, it means generally accepted accounting *practices*. In most countries, GAAP is simply a long, haphazard list of rules that usually are not even principles. Furthermore, whether the rules are enforced depends on the quality of the auditing.

The Significance of GAAP Differences. Differences among various types of GAAP have great significance for financial analysts. Consider some of the implications. Different versions of GAAP

- may record revenue sooner,
- may cause quality of earnings to differ,
- may boost revenue with one-time gains,
- allow big-bath accounting,
- do not require disclosure of all liabilities, and
- can cause expenses to be shifted to different periods.

Another reason to care about differences in GAAP is that bad accounting tends to promote bad business decisions. Transactions that are not economical or profitable can be reported in a way that makes them appear to be profitable. The consequences can be severe. For example, if an insurance company uses bad accounting, the next step is mispricing of insurance products and the third step is failure.

Differences in accounting practices reduce the comparability of financial numbers. The problem is particularly serious in analyzing an industry. For example, in the automotive industry, comparing manufacturers in Germany with manufacturers in Italy and France is extremely difficult. Assessing such items as free cash flow, value of assets, or even liquidity can also be a challenge.

Figure 1 shows differences between IAS and U.S. GAAP for 32 companies in 1999. Non-U.S. companies that file financial statements in the United States need to present a GAAP reconciliation. They start with their IAS income and reconcile to the U.S. GAAP income. They need to complete the same task for their IAS equity. In Figure 1, each dot represents a company. The horizontal axis shows the difference between U.S. GAAP equity and IAS equity, and the vertical axis shows the difference between U.S. GAAP income and IAS income. For example, one company's U.S. GAAP equity is about 55 percent lower than its IAS equity. Another company's U.S. GAAP equity is about 50 percent higher than its IAS equity. On the income axis, one company's U.S. GAAP income is roughly 80 percent higher than its IAS income and another company's U.S. GAAP is about 95 percent lower. Clearly, the differences between IAS and U.S. GAAP can have profound significance.

Consider another potential problem: If a company's U.S. GAAP reconciling items are negative one year, then one would expect them to become positive in later years, with differences averaging out to zero in the long run. Such an outcome would be expected were it not for the fact that certain items of income are never charged to the income statement under one GAAP or the other. So, if a company using IAS revalues its fixed assets, it will account for the revaluation in equity but never show the revaluation in its income, not even when it sells the asset, whereas under U.S. GAAP, it will always be forced to show the increase in value in income on sale of the asset.

Certain provisions in IAS and U.S. GAAP ensure that the lifetime income of companies is not identical under the two systems simply because part of an income or expense may be diverted to equity directly. In short, even if companies have an incentive to make sure that few differences occur between their IAS and U.S. GAAP financial statements, the differences will still be highly significant. **Table 1** shows the number of reconciling differences observed in different reporting categories among the 32 companies depicted in Figure 1. Although these data reflect differences only between U.S. GAAP and IAS, a similar chart could be created for comparison of any two accounting frameworks. Discrepancies in such areas as deferred taxation, pensions and other postretirement benefits, stock-based compensation plans, goodwill, and investments are not surprising. More striking is that 13 companies reported differences regarding tangible fixed assets—and sizable differences in most cases.

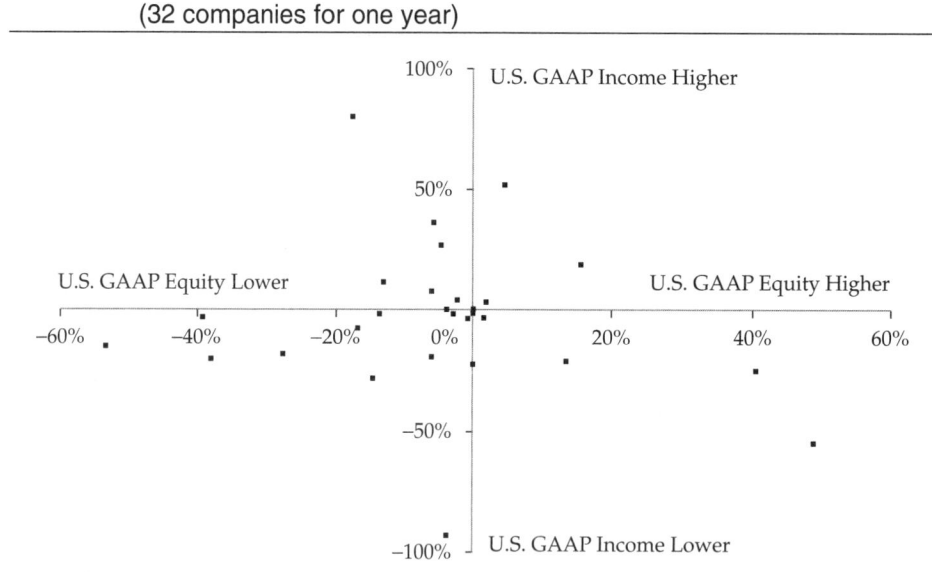

Figure 1. Differences between IAS and U.S. GAAP
(32 companies for one year)

Table 1. Differences between IAS and U.S. GAAP

Reporting Category	Number of Differences
Deferred taxation	21
Intangible assets	15
Tangible fixed assets	13
Pensions and other post-retirement benefits	11
Stock-based compensation plans	11
Goodwill	8
Capital instruments and debt	7
Capitalization of interest	7
Investments	7
Accounting for associates and joint ventures	6
Business combinations	6
Dividends	5
Financial instruments	5
Revenue recognition	5
Sale and leaseback agreements	5
Restructuring and redundancy costs	3
Foreign exchange gains and losses	2
Other	11
Total number of differences (32 companies)	148

Reconciling the Numbers

This section deals with some of the most infamous types of differences among various accounting standards. I will offer an overview of the differences, the quality of the numbers, their impact on financial statements, and my recommendations (if I have any). Seven areas in particular are notorious for GAAP differences: business combinations and goodwill, consolidation and special purpose entities (SPEs), leasing, pension accounting, deferred taxation, share-based payments (stock options), and revenue recognition.

Business Combinations and Goodwill. Three approaches are available for accounting for business combinations. The first approach is purchase accounting, in which an acquired entity's assets and liabilities are recorded at their fair value with the difference recorded as goodwill. Goodwill can be accounted for in one of two ways: the IAS/U.K. GAAP way, in which goodwill is amortized over its life (whatever that may be), or the U.S. GAAP way, in which goodwill is assumed to hold its value over time (the company is required to do an annual impairment test, and if the goodwill does lose value, a charge to income is made to reflect the loss in value).

Currently, IAS and U.K. GAAP also allow the pooling-of-interests method of accounting for business combinations. (This method is no longer allowed under U.S. GAAP.) This approach means that when one company acquires another company, the two balance sheets are combined, book values are not adjusted, and historical costs are carried over. The effect of this approach is pervasive. For example, consider the implication of pooling of interests under U.K. GAAP. A large company can acquire a small company that owned property bought in 1920. Under pooling of interests, if that property was sold three years after the business combination, a huge gain would result because the property was recorded at historical cost. A more realistic accounting assessment would acknowledge that the large company paid full price for the property at the time the small company was acquired and that, from the acquirer's point of view, no substantial gain occurred.

Some European countries (e.g., France and the Netherlands) have, or have had, a third approach: a hybrid accounting method, also called purchase accounting. This method, however, does not revalue the assets or liabilities acquired or account for goodwill. The difference in the book value of the assets and liabilities acquired is charged to equity. All three methods—purchase accounting, pooling of interests, and the hybrid method—give rise to enormous differences in how business combinations are reported.

Analysts should be aware of three major weaknesses that purchase accounting encompasses: subjective judgment associated with the valuation of assets and liabilities, provisions for future liabilities whose potential for subsequent reversal creates earnings quality issues, and amortization of goodwill. The revaluation of assets and liabilities is a highly subjective, time-consuming process that opens the door to a wide range of value interpretations. For example, appraisals for in-process R&D are often needed. How does one value that asset?

Typically, in the case of a business combination, the acquiring company sets up provisions for various events—a potential tax claim or liability. Five or six years down the road, the company may discover that it has been overly cautious and can release some of these provisions. The result is that business combinations tend to give rise to accounting profit, not real profit, for years following the combination. For analysts charged with assessing the quality of a company's earnings, it is critically important to recognize that the quality of earnings is definitely lower for serial acquirers than for companies with simple organic growth—mainly because of the bias in the accounting rules that allows acquirers to set themselves up for future accounting profits, as opposed to economic profits.

The amortization of goodwill under purchase accounting does not reflect the change in value of the business; that is, the loss in value of goodwill is not accurately recognized by amortization of goodwill. U.S. GAAP attempts to correct for this pitfall by requiring an annual impairment test on the amount of annual amortization expense. The problem with impairment testing, however, is that, in effect, an impairment test is a valuation. Unless the impairment test is extremely rigorous, it is worse than useless.

Business combinations are easy to spot, but the accounting effects that such combinations trigger are not so easy to spot. When analyzing a company that has acquired other companies, analysts would be wise to ask more questions about the accounting, valuations, and revaluations associated with the acquisition.

Consolidation and SPEs. Consolidation and SPEs constitute a major source of GAAP differences. Accounting for consolidation is theoretically straightforward. If the balance sheets and any transactions between the entities are eliminated, a parent company and its subsidiaries are combined (added together). The result is a consolidated balance sheet. What is not straightforward is why some subsidiaries under various European GAAP frameworks are included on the consolidated financial statements and others are not.

In Europe, the rationale for choosing one company and not another for consolidated reporting varies. A typical reason for not including a subsidiary is that the subsidiary is in a completely different line of business. But if a manufacturing company does not consolidate its banking subsidiary, a huge chunk of the parent's assets and liabilities will not be reported. Another reason for excluding a subsidiary from consolidated financial statements is that the parent company has entered discussions to sell the subsidiary; thus, the subsidiary has effectively been eliminated and consolidation is not necessary. Obviously, such treatment can have an enormous impact on balance sheet ratios and reported income. Subsidiaries and SPEs that are loss making, have start-up activities, are highly geared, or have enormous balance sheet liabilities are often not consolidated, which enhances reported numbers significantly.

Under IAS and U.K. GAAP, however, companies are required to consolidate all subsidiaries and SPEs. U.S. GAAP also requires consolidation of all subsidiaries and SPEs, except for those exempted in the accounting regulations. For example, Statement of Financial Accounting Standards (SFAS) No. 140, *Accounting for Transfers and Servicing of Financial Assets and Extinguishments of Liabilities*, allows exclusion of qualifying SPEs—those used for securitizations.[1] SPEs are also excluded from consolidation if a third party has an investment of at least 3 percent in the entity. This treatment is commonly used for leasing structures, debt factoring, and financing of subsidiaries, as well as many other types of transactions.

I have few recommendations to offer in this area. Analysts need to be aware that not all companies consolidate all of their subsidiaries and not all companies consolidate all of their SPEs. A significant part of a company's business may not be included in its financial statements, which makes proper analysis extremely difficult. Analysts must always try to determine whether a parent company has entered into any special leasing securitizations or other structured finance transactions with a subsidiary because such activities are likely to have a huge impact, which is not always obvious, on the company's financial position.

Leasing. Accounting for leasing transactions has always been controversial. In the United States, about 13 or 14 different financial accounting standards deal with leasing. In Europe, far less guidance exists. The most popular treatment of leasing is to capitalize only those leases that will transfer legal title of the asset. Thus, in France and Germany, companies show leased assets on the balance sheet only if they will actually acquire the asset based on the terms of the lease. This practice means that getting assets off the balance sheet is as simple as eliminating the clause in the lease contract that transfers title.

Under IAS, however, companies need to capitalize leased assets if the lease payments exceed 90 percent of the asset's net present value, as well as if the lease transaction meets a few more conditions. The 90 percent requirement leaves a lot of room for playing games. A typical trick is to structure a lease with payments equal to 89.9 percent of the leased asset's net present value so that the lease escapes capitalization treatment. Typically, we sign off on this treatment because it is the market standard and a generally accepted practice, although it is not particularly good accounting.

The problem for analysts with off-balance-sheet leasing is that significant assets of the company, significant parts of the business, are not captured in the financial statements, yet the company is still exposed to the risks of these off-balance-sheet assets. For example, if a company enters into a 15-year lease for an office building but finds it does not need the building after 5 years because its business has collapsed, the company has a significant liability that is not apparent on its balance sheet. The main advantage of off-balance-sheet leasing is that it improves the company's balance sheet ratios.

Again, I can offer few recommendations in regard to leasing. Current GAAP frameworks are definitely flawed because they allow companies to

---

[1] A summary of SFAS No. 140 (issued September 2000) can be found at www.fasb.org/st/summary/stsum140.shtml.

leave significant assets and risks off the balance sheet as a result of the 90 percent capitalization threshold. Analysts must determine whether companies have such leases and how important the leases are to the overall financial health of the companies.

Pension Accounting. Pension accounting has always been a challenge. In one respect, however, it is not difficult—actuarial calculations determine the pension liability.

A number of different methods of pension accounting exist. Under IAS, like U.S. GAAP, the net assets of pension funds must be recognized and actuarial gains and losses must be amortized. A pension fund has enormous assets and liabilities, and netting these large numbers produces a relatively small number that is subject to enormous volatility. Accountants do not like enormous volatility; therefore, both IAS and U.S. GAAP give companies the ability to smooth volatility, as Patricia McConnell describes.[2]

This method has its detractors, who disagree with the practice of reporting pension assets when the pension fund may be in deficit, or vice versa, which misrepresents the net position of the pension plan. Some believe that a company's balance sheets should immediately reflect its net pension asset or net pension deficit. To this end, the new U.K. GAAP standard, Financial Reporting Standard (FRS) 17, requires a company to recognize the net assets of its pension fund immediately. If a pension fund has a huge investment loss, the investment loss will be charged to the equity of the sponsoring company in the period in which it occurs. Companies in the United Kingdom are not particularly happy with FRS 17 because it can result in a tremendous amount of volatility from one period to the next.

The extent of the volatility depends to a large degree on the industry of the reporting company. For example, for companies in the steel industry, with pension funds that often have about 200,000 retirees and 30,000 active members, the amount of volatility depends on the total number—not just the active number—of people in the pension scheme. Such pension plans tend to generate volatility that has nothing to do with current employees or the business. Similarly, many airline pension funds have assets that are well in excess of five times the market capitalization of the sponsoring airline.

In continental Europe, pension accounting is easy because companies completely ignore their pension funds. Of course, off-balance-sheet treatment of pension plans improves balance sheet ratios and also gives companies an opportunity to take a pension holiday (a common practice in continental Europe). Pension holidays are periods in which a company does not contribute to its pension fund because the pension fund has a surplus that is not shown in the company's financial statements. Essentially, a company can decide at any time to skip contributions to the pension fund for a given year and take a pension holiday. In some cases, companies can demand a refund from the pension fund and show the refund as a credit on the income statement. Both practices are becoming less common but are still around. The off-balance-sheet treatment of pensions ignores the significant liability that can reside in pension funds, and it also creates the potential for surprise gains and losses on the pension fund assets, which can cause great volatility in reported income.

Perhaps the ultimate pension valuation challenge is the phenomenon that many European companies operate under: pay-as-you-go pension schemes. The pension plans do not own any assets; retirement benefits are simply paid from operating income in the year they are due to the retiree. And a company accounts for a pension liability only when an employee retires. This approach makes for extremely bad accounting but is accepted practice in many countries. When making comparisons between countries, analysts need to make adjustments for such practices because the numbers involved are substantial.

Under U.S. GAAP, pension accounting is still fairly easy because the assets are reported not at market value but at a weighted average that trails market value. The net pension asset is also based on a smoothed liability, so the result is a double-smoothing mechanism, which can be handy for a company in forecasting its net income.

An important factor to consider when analyzing a company is the kind of benefits companies are providing to their employees. Under accounting frameworks in which pension liabilities are not reported, it is easy for a company to be generous. If, for example, a company wants to avoid a strike, it can simply give extra pension benefits to its employees. The extra benefits (pension liabilities) do not show up in the company's financial statements, and the effects of a higher pension liability will not be apparent until years later, which makes the analyst's job a bit tricky.

Deferred Taxation. Deferred taxation is frequently a stumbling block in valuation because financial statements rarely provide enough information for analysts to glean any insight into what caused the deferred taxation and why the amount should not be double or half the amount reported.

---
[2] Please see Ms. McConnell's presentation in this proceedings.

There are several ways of accounting for deferred taxes. In continental Europe, one method is simply to account for the tax that the company must pay on the current year's profit and ignore any future tax effects. If the company has a tax asset that is not tax deductible in the current year, the company does not account for any of the future tax effects associated with that asset because they do not affect the current year. This practice is common in most of Europe, and it is not a problem if the financial statements are tax linked because companies typically do not have much deferred tax anyway. For international conglomerates or business combinations, however, enormous differences can occur between the book value of assets and the tax base of the same assets.

In the United Kingdom, accounting for deferred taxes is slightly different from that followed in continental Europe. U.K. GAAP's reporting requirements for deferred taxes are driven by the income statement. If income is taxed in a period different from the period in which it is reported in the financial statements, companies need to account for the deferred tax. Companies in the United Kingdom also must account for deferred tax on business combinations and on revaluations. They do not have to account for all deferred tax, however, so be aware that some tax liabilities may be ignored on financial statements.

Similarly, under IAS and U.S. GAAP, companies can ignore certain tax liabilities as long as the liabilities meet the conditions defined in the governing accounting standard. For example, companies are allowed to ignore certain tax assets and liabilities, such as the deferred tax on goodwill and the deferred tax on certain undistributed profits in foreign subsidiaries. Normally, however, under IAS and GAAP, companies account for all tax that they must pay in the current year, the next year, and so forth, and they also account for all tax liabilities and tax assets that relate to any item on their balance sheet.

The point to take home is that significant tax liabilities may remain unrecognized under GAAP in certain countries. The first step is to understand the accounting policy for deferred tax. Unfortunately, even if analysts understand the accounting policy perfectly, financial statements rarely provide enough information to allow a recalculation in accordance with another form of GAAP. The only way to find those numbers is to request them directly from the company in question.

Analysts should also remember that business combinations or revaluations can give rise to enormous deferred tax liabilities, so a business combination that does not give rise to deferred tax liabilities should be suspect. Finally, very helpful to analysts is a deferred tax reconciliation found in the footnotes to the financial statements. The reconciliation is between the statutory tax rate and the actual tax rate, as shown in the income statement. If a company is based in a country with a statutory tax rate of 40 percent and the income statement shows a tax rate of only 32 percent, the reconciliation explains the 8 percent difference. A typical explanation would be that income earned in another country is taxed at a lower rate or that certain expenses are not deductible in another country in which the company is operating.

Analysts should review the individual items in the tax-rate reconciliation statement and determine whether they properly belong in the reconciliation; some will not (e.g., sometimes, the economic life of assets differs between GAAPs, which is not what one would expect). Also, the reconciliation needs to be presented for two years. The underlying aim of all deferred tax accounting is to show a stable tax rate. If the tax rate last year was 32 percent, then next year it should also be 32 percent, or very close. A two-year reconciliation shows any tax charges that rise or fall by 5 or 10 percent from year to year. Those fluctuations should raise doubts about the company's deferred tax calculation.

Share-Based Payments. The difficulty in accounting for share-based payments is typically not related to the calculation of the value of the options being issued; many valuation firms/appraisers can do that. Some room for game playing does exist in valuations, especially with the assumptions regarding volatility and dividend policy, but the value typically falls in a range between 100 and 150. With share-based payments, the discount rate is unimportant, or at least relatively unimportant, because the valuation models are more sensitive to dividend and volatility assumptions.

Share-based payments can be accounted for in four ways. The first method is to ignore the subject completely, with the attitude that shares have no cost but the cost of the paper on which they are printed. This approach is typically used in continental Europe.

The second method, the U.K. GAAP approach, is to account for certain types of share-based compensation. For example, if a company issues shares to its employees but also promises to buy back the shares within three weeks, the transaction is similar to a cash plan and the company will account for the charge.

The U.S. GAAP method accounts for employee stock options based on the intrinsic value of the option, completely ignoring the time value of the option. This method is not good accounting, but it is accepted practice in the United States.

The final method, the SFAS No. 123 (*Accounting for Stock-Based Compensation*) approach, is to account for stock options by using a proper option valuation model (i.e., Black and Scholes).[3]

Today, employee stock options are part of the cost of doing business. The debate in accounting has always centered on the question of whether stock options are a cost to the issuing entity. Clearly, stock options are not a cost to the issuing entity because their cost is worth no more than the paper on which the shares are printed. But stock options are a cost to shareholders because the value of their shares will be diluted and they will lose money. But what is meant by the term "entity"? Are the investors and their concerns part of the entity or is the entity solely the company proper? The lengthy debate has finally resulted in the conclusion that entities should account for the cost of share-based compensation, but the first step in following through on this conclusion has to be a definition of the entity.

One of the quirks of share-based compensation is that when employees exercise their stock options, they pay a tax on the compensation received. In the United States, the company also gets a tax credit for options that have been exercised. According to traditional European accounting, even though a company does not account for stock options, it gets a tax credit when employees exercise the options and it must account for that credit in its profit-and-loss statement.

Research into the effectiveness of stock options as compensation has tended to show that if employees are given stock options worth, for example, $200,000, they perceive the value of their stock options to be somewhere between $50,000 and $100,000. Thus, from the shareholders' point of view, share-based payments are an inefficient form of compensation. This is probably a good reason why companies should not be using employee stock options as a form of compensation. But from a company's point of view, stock options are noncash payments. Regardless of how employee stock options are viewed and accounted for—or not—analysts must be attuned to the fact that the options exist and that they may or may not affect the company's financial position and financial statements.

Revenue Recognition. Revenue recognition of tangible goods and assets depends on either delivery of the asset, invoicing of the asset, or some other event, such as regulatory approval. The nature of the event differs from country to country, industry to industry, and company to company. Thus, when analysts examine revenue recognition, they always need to ask the companies exactly what practice they are following, because nothing can be taken for granted. Also, many different methods for recognizing revenue exist, such as the completed-contract method, under which profits are recognized when all obligations have been fulfilled, and the percentage-of-completion method, which is used in the construction industry. And Patricia McConnell[4] raises the issue of allocation of revenues in multielement transactions. How should we account for individual components of a contract?

In regard to revenue recognition, the accounting profession does not have any good solutions. Certain industries are notorious for having revenue spikes. For example, most of the quarterly revenue may come in the third month of the quarter. When dealing with such a revenue pattern, analysts need to examine the revenue recognition method used by the company, because in such cases, extending that third month by one day or two days can cause a significant increase in quarterly revenue. Likewise, recognizing revenue for contracts that have been signed, rather than for products that have been delivered, will significantly enhance a company's reported performance.

Conclusion

Differences among accounting standard regimes can have a significant impact on the financial reporting of companies and can make the comparison of companies extremely complicated and uncertain, particularly for the purposes of industry analysis. In some cases, the nature of the differences makes ascertaining the truth behind the numbers impossible. Often, the best analysts can do is to be aware of the potential hazards and proceed with extreme caution. Analysts who understand the accounting standards and the different practices followed in multiple countries and industries have the best chance of identifying and avoiding suspect companies.

Furthermore, analysts should note that a number of countries have "conservative" accounting policies. In this sense, conservative means that when a company is doing well, it understates revenue; when it is collapsing, it overstates revenue. I oppose conservative accounting policies because they mean shifting profits from one period to another, with the result that the market gets information too late, denying the opportunity for early identification of deteriorating companies.

---

[3] A summary of SFAS No. 123 (issued October 1995) can be found at www.fasb.org/st/summary/stsum123.shtml.

[4] Please see Ms. McConnell's presentation in this proceedings.

Question and Answer Session
Pieter Dekker

Question: Which countries have the most egregious accounting practices?

Dekker: Particularly poor accounting can be found in Germany, Italy, and, to some extent, France, mainly because companies in those countries don't consolidate all their subsidiaries. If a company does not consolidate its subsidiaries, sales to those subsidiaries show up in the top line of the financial statements. For example, with a car manufacturer that has a financing subsidiary that leases cars and provides operating leases to end users, if the parent company doesn't consolidate the financing subsidiary, any sale to the subsidiary will end up as 100 percent revenue, even though the car manufacturer is not merely a car manufacturer.

Question: What percentage of the companies in a major European index, such as the S&P Europe 350, report under IAS?

Dekker: Currently, the percentage is tiny because reporting under IAS is not allowed in most countries in Europe. European entities need to comply with the requirements of the 4th and 7th European (EU) Accounting Directives, which effectively preclude reporting under IAS. But beginning in 2005, a number of companies in Europe will be required to report under IAS, a significant change that will lead to better financial reporting.

Question: Will a one-time period of poor earnings occur with the advent of IAS?

Dekker: No. Companies that make the transition to IAS at the end of 2005 will restate their equity in accordance with IAS back to the beginning of 2004, so there will be a reconciling difference between ending equity in 2003 and beginning equity in 2004.

Question: What sort of adjustment should investors expect?

Dekker: The International Accounting Standards Board's current exposure draft of the IAS allows companies to grandfather quite a few items (i.e., not restate previous transactions). Nonetheless, companies will not be allowed to grandfather securitizations, leases, pensions, and a number of other items.

Question: How will financial statements be affected?

Dekker: Much depends on the companies in question as to how their financial statements will change. The main impact will be more items on the balance sheet. Under IAS, more earnings volatility will occur because fair value accounting is required for a number of items, such as financial instruments. The change also means that significant liabilities related to pension plans and leases will be put on the balance sheet. Under IAS, companies will not be able to manipulate earnings to the extent that they can under their current governing GAAP. Provision accounting will effectively be outlawed.

Question: Is the main impact of the switch to IAS a question of volatility and bigger balance sheets, rather than necessarily a reduction in earnings?

Dekker: The impact is difficult to predict. For example, IAS and U.S. GAAP are fairly similar frameworks. But if we plotted the differences between IAS and U.S. GAAP for a single year, as in Figure 1, the differences would still be enormous, and the differences are not highly predictable. In Figure 1, the companies are dispersed among all four quadrants. Most companies that followed sensible accounting practices before a switch to IAS will end up somewhere in the middle of the figure. The companies that practiced more creative accounting before they applied IAS will be outliers and will experience a significant impact on income and equity.

Question: Which country in the EU will have the largest adjustments to make under IAS?

Dekker: Germany will face major adjustments. For example, in Germany, leases are recognized only if legal ownership of the assets is acquired. Also, pension accounting there is below par. France, Italy, and Austria will have similar problems.

Question: Would you discuss some of the issues associated with lease accounting?

Dekker: Lease accounting has always been a big issue. Under a U.K./U.S. GAAP framework, if the net present value of lease payments exceeds 90 percent of the fair value of the assets, the lease needs to be capitalized, or if the lease term exceeds 75 percent of the economic life of the asset, the lease needs to be capitalized. Basically, companies are playing with all of these rules. If a lessor is selling a lease to a lessee, the lessor will work around all of these conditions and will structure the lease in such a way that it becomes a borderline operating lease so that the transaction can be off balance sheet. Another issue of concern with respect to leasing is that quite a few leases are missold. For example, many synthetic leases involve SPEs that lease the assets from the parent company as off-balance-sheet leases or structures, such as sale and "operating leasebacks." Such products are never off balance sheet, but lessors tend to market them as off-balance-sheet products in the hope of finding a gullible client or auditor—and they get away with it.

Question: How can tax charges be subject to management control?

Dekker: If you account for deferred tax, it is subject to management control. A good example is deferred taxes related to foreign subsidiaries. Under current IAS and U.S. standards, you don't have to account for those deferred tax charges if you do not intend to distribute the retained earnings that would give rise to the tax charges. If your intent changes and the retained earnings will be distributed the following year, you do need to account immediately for the deferred taxes; in this way, management can exert control over tax charges.

Question: Is goodwill tax deductible under any accounting standards?

Dekker: Goodwill's tax deductibility depends not on accounting standards but on tax legislation and the jurisdiction in which the company operates. A few jurisdictions allow a company to deduct some of the goodwill that has been paid in calculating the company's tax liability, but differences exist in the amount of goodwill that is applicable for tax and accounting purposes. The goodwill for tax purposes may be much lower or higher than the accounting goodwill.

Question: If a company buys 20 percent of a company and generates goodwill and buys another 10 percent at a later date on the basis of a lower value, does the amortization of the goodwill from the first acquisition have to be accelerated or can it still be amortized over a longer period?

Dekker: The answer depends on the accounting framework under which the company is reporting. Under current U.S. GAAP, if a company buys 25 percent and pays X amount of goodwill and if it buys another 10 percent, it needs to compare the value of the 35 percent stake with the carrying amount of the goodwill, and the goodwill may or may not be impaired. Under other accounting frameworks, companies typically can amortize the goodwill and not recognize the loss on the initial tranche, despite the fact that the second tranche is significantly cheaper; thus, companies tend to accumulate goodwill with successive partial acquisitions of the same company.

Valuing Hypergrowth/High-Uncertainty Companies—A Practical Approach

Barney H. Wilson
Chief Investment Officer
Lincoln Equity Management, LLC
Chicago

> Valuation of hypergrowth or high-uncertainty companies poses difficulties for the traditional present value model, particularly because of the model's sensitivity to the discount rate and fade rate and the potential for disparate outcomes. Combining adjusted DCF analysis with scenario analysis can mitigate some of these problems, but it is extremely time consuming. For everyday analysis, a simple valuation framework, which involves using forecast forward P/E at the end of a company's hypergrowth period and estimated appreciation in stock price during the hypergrowth phase, can be an effective and less time-consuming alternative.

The concepts I will discuss were originally designed for high-growth technology companies, but they apply to all high-growth, high-risk, or what I call "high-uncertainty" companies. One of the most difficult challenges for investors in the late 1990s was using the discounted cash flow (DCF) method to value tech companies that had revenues growing at 50–60 percent a year. In the current environment, although no company is growing so rapidly, many are experiencing a high degree of uncertainty as to what two- and three-year-forward cash flows will be. I will comment on the traditional present value, or DCF, model and will highlight the primary areas of difficulty in using it to value hypergrowth/high-uncertainty companies.

Throughout this presentation, bear in mind that my experience as a buy-side research analyst informs my valuation work. I spend the vast majority of my time conducting classic fundamental research—meeting with companies' management, customers, suppliers, and competitors; constructing financial models; and building spreadsheets. I focus on one stock at a time. I have found from experience that the DCF method is most powerful when used in conjunction with scenario analysis, which focuses on a company's risk–reward potential rather than a point estimate of value. I will share with you a simple, nuts-and-bolts valuation framework that can be used on an everyday basis.

Traditional Present Value Method

In the traditional present value method, the analyst projects a company's cash flows and discounts them back to the present in order to obtain a fair value estimate of the company's stock. The concept of valuing a stock based on the discounted value of its cash flows is logical because it keeps the focus on cash so as to avoid accounting distortions. Furthermore, the DCF method is a systematic and disciplined approach that avoids the comparable-company valuations that were prevalent in 1999 and 2000. For example, some analysts argued that because stocks of communications equipment companies were trading at, on average, 70 times forward earnings, a communication equipment stock trading at 50 times forward earnings was cheap. The focus on present value of future cash flows prevents analysts from falling into that particular trap. The method incorporates risk factors, future investment needs, and return on capital as critical elements of valuation.

Although the approach is logical, systematic, and disciplined, it does not work well for many hypergrowth/high-uncertainty companies, especially the most volatile ones. Under the DCF method, if a company is growing rapidly, its stock usually will appear to be "expensive," and if the company's fundamentals weaken, its stock can appear to be "cheap." Thus, the method tends to invite sale or purchase of the stock at precisely the wrong time.

Anecdotal evidence of this phenomenon abounds. For example, in early 1999, when the fundamentals started to accelerate for some of the "new economy" companies, such as Oracle Corporation, Cisco Systems, and Sun Microsystems, the stocks appeared too expensive to buy, especially if an analyst used a high discount rate when valuing the operating cash flows of the company. Many investors avoided these stocks while their prices were rising. They stayed out of the stocks during 1999 and early 2000 and watched from the sidelines as the stocks appreciated 50–100 percent or more. Then, in late 2000, when the companies' fundamentals started to weaken and the stocks had a meaningful pullback, many investors stepped in to buy the stocks. They thought the stocks were now cheap enough to buy, but the stock prices dropped much more as the fundamentals weakened further.

DCF Shortcomings

I have identified three areas of difficulty in using the DCF method for hypergrowth/high-uncertainty companies: the range for the critical variables, the discount rate, and the fade rate.

Range. The critical variables that drive a fair value estimate for a traditional company—revenue growth, operating margin, working capital growth, capital expenditures, and return on capital—all have a reasonable range of expected values. For more traditional companies, analysts generally can have a high level of confidence that their cash flow and earnings estimates based on these variables will be relatively close to the actual numbers that the company delivers.

For traditional companies with low risk—that is, companies with basic business drivers that are not highly volatile (a beer company, for example)—analysts can expect a normal probability distribution, the familiar bell-shaped curve, for the range of values for each of the critical variables and thus for the companies' cash flows. The peak of the bell (the normal distribution) is the base case, the weighted average of all possible outcomes, and the highest-probability case. The tails of the distribution represent the highly unlikely outcomes and are not of significant size. As a company's risk increases, the width of the bell (that is, the standard deviation) increases because the critical variables have greater variability. But even for a medium- or high-risk traditional company, the distribution is normal for the range of possible values of the critical valuation variables.

For a hypergrowth/high-uncertainty company, however, the reasonable range of critical valuation variables is much wider and the probability distribution of the outcomes is *not* normal. In contrast to a traditional, low-risk company, analysts cannot have a high confidence level in their one- to two-year projections for a hypergrowth/high-uncertainty company's revenues. Actual revenues can deviate from the projections by 50 percent or more.

Consider the example of Marconi Corporation, a U.K. communication equipment provider. In April 2000, some sell-side analysts' forecasts for the fiscal year (FY) ending March 2003 were around €8.5 billion. By October 2002, the forecasts for the same FY were revised to €2.5 billion—a 71 percent decrease in an 18-month period. This dramatic change from forecast to actual is typical of high-growth, high-risk companies.

In the United States today, the revenue estimates for many hypergrowth, high-tech companies have dropped 90 percent or more from the original forecasts made one to two years earlier; in fact, a number of companies that previously were forecast to generate hundreds of millions of dollars in revenue are out of business completely. For companies with a high uncertainty level, it is sometimes the case for actual revenues to be zero percent of the original forecast revenues. The base-case forecast for such companies has a low probability of occurring, and there is a high probability that actual cash flows will be in the tails of the distribution. The distribution is bimodal and far from normal; it is a wide, inverted distribution.

Discount Rate. Another difficulty with the DCF model is determining the correct discount rate for hypergrowth/high-uncertainty companies. This problem relates to the wide range of potential outcomes.

Although there are many ways to determine the discount rate, one of the most popular is to start with the risk-free rate and add a market risk premium and a company-specific risk premium. For a low-risk, traditional company with a normal probability distribution, using the lowest discount rate, or a slightly higher one to account for a higher standard deviation, makes sense. For a company with a bimodal distribution, however, the discount rate framework breaks down. Many value-oriented investors make the mistake of increasing the discount rate on tech stocks because of their high volatility. But if the discount rate is too high, the highest-quality, best-operating tech stocks appear to be too expensive to buy.

Fade Rate. Determining the correct fade rate for hypergrowth, high-tech companies is an exercise in which satisfactory precision is nearly impossible.

In a DCF model, the fade rate is the rate at which the growth of a company, after the initial forecast period, converges to the default terminal growth rate. For most companies (including high-uncertainty companies that do not have a high growth rate), valuation is not sensitive to this variable, but for companies growing at a rate of 50–60 percent a year, valuation is very sensitive to this variable.

In 1999, when I was valuing Amazon.com, its revenue growth rate was well in excess of 50 percent a year. The base-case fade rate in my model was 10 percent until the later-stage growth rate was applied. If I changed the fade rate from 10 percent to 12 percent, the fair value dropped 40 percent. That is simply the way the math works: When the change is from 50 percent growth to single-digit growth, the rate of the fade has a large impact on the cash flows. Given that the analyst is guessing whether a 10 percent or a 12 percent fade is the right number, it is a weakness of the DCF model that the fair value is so sensitive to this variable.

DCF Adjustments

Two adjustments can be made to address the difficulties in applying a DCF analysis to hypergrowth/high-uncertainty companies. First, I conceptually distinguish between the hypergrowth or high-uncertainty growth period and the subsequent growth period, and second, I use scenario analysis. In my view, valuations of high-tech companies, or any hypergrowth/high-uncertainty company, must be based on the company's risk–reward potential, not merely on a point estimate of value.

Separating the growth phases allows for the use of different discount rates for different growth periods. It also facilitates scenario analysis and reduces the importance of the fade rate.

The scenario analysis process, which I will illustrate, is as follows. First, do a base-case scenario and then do upside- and downside-case scenarios. The DCF analysis begins after the target company's hypergrowth/high-uncertainty growth phase is estimated to end. Using a relatively stable business model, the output of the DCF analysis (the expected value at the end of the hypergrowth/high-uncertainty phase) is discounted back at the subjective desired rate of return for holding this type of stock.

Example. Consider the case of XYZ Company. The upside-case scenario forecasts revenue growth of 15 percent for the next several years, with modest operating margin expansion. The downside-case scenario forecasts a revenue contraction of 5 percent for the next several years and margin degradation. As with most hypergrowth/high-uncertainty companies, the upside scenario easily has more than double the profits of the downside scenario, and both scenarios are equally plausible.

In this case, the key inputs to the DCF model are the current revenue level, the projected revenue growth rate, and the estimate of modestly increasing operating margins. As I stated earlier, I begin the DCF analysis after the high-growth period. Today, that means that I am starting the DCF model in 2005. I use a relatively moderate discount rate to avoid the problems associated with using one that is too high. So, if the output of the DCF model in the upside scenario is $28 a share, I discount that back to the present at a rate of 20 percent (a rate that compensates fairly for risk, in my estimation), which produces a current fair value estimate of $20 a share.

If the outcome of my three scenarios is an upside value of $23 a share, a base-case value of $11 a share, and a downside value of $5 a share, then the next step is to assign a probability to each of those scenarios—60 percent, 20 percent, and 20 percent, respectively. In assigning probabilities, the analyst's judgment, namely his or her view of the industry structure and likely developments for the company and industry, plays a large role. It is tempting to calculate the expected value of the three scenario values based on the probabilities of each, which is $15 a share, but that is not meaningful. In this approach, the table of possible outcomes is what has meaning and value, which requires thinking in terms of probabilities and magnitudes. Instead of focusing on a single expected stock value, analysts should consider the magnitude of the upside value and the probability that the upside case will come to pass, and they should do a similar analysis for the downside case.

The scenario approach requires a different analytical vocabulary that produces a more focused, stronger argument in support of a particular valuation. An analyst's opinion is often expressed in the following vernacular: The stock price is $13 a share, the target price is $15 a share, and the stock has a high degree of risk. Compare that with the following: The upside scenario for this stock has a 60 percent chance of occurring, and for this scenario, the fair value is $20 a share, which is 50 percent above the current stock price of $13 a share. The latter argument is more specific than the first because it relays the same data—but in terms of risk–reward probabilities and magnitudes. Such an argument is more compelling and provides the stimulus to do further work—to say, for example, that more likely than not, the upside scenario will happen and the magnitude of the upside is significant.

Advantages. Adjusted DCF analysis combined with scenario analysis is an approach that allows analysts to significantly reduce the sensitivity of the modeling process to the discount rate and fade rate and eliminates the need to take the average of disparate possible outcomes. It not only directs analysts' focus to probabilities and magnitudes and reduces the false impression of precision; it is also flexible. The importance of flexibility became particularly evident during the tech-stock bubble. When many investors who genuinely cared about valuation found that their valuation method was not providing adequate guidance, they either abandoned valuation altogether or switched to a non-cash-flow-based valuation method. A less-rigid valuation method would have been of greater support during this unusual period.

This approach is also useful for interpreting breaking news or a sharply moving stock price. To the extent that an analyst has a strong conviction about the likely downside case and upside case, he or she is more likely to be able to take advantage of any short-term move in the price of the stock. Executing the scenario analysis approach, the analyst is forced to make judgments about the magnitude and the probability of both the upside and the downside for a company and its stock price.

A Simple Valuation Framework

Scenario analysis is beneficial, but it is time-consuming to do three full DCF models for every company being analyzed. Therefore, I use a shorthand framework on a daily basis. The basic inputs are the same as those for a DCF model: growth rates, operating margins, tax rate, and share count. A second input is the predicted 12-month forward P/E for the stock, calculated at what is estimated to be the end of its hypergrowth/high-uncertainty phase. A third input is the stock appreciation required during the hypergrowth/high-uncertainty phase.

Although the legitimacy of P/E as a valuation tool is controversial, I view P/E as a surrogate for the output of a DCF model. I use a number based on operating cash flow to represent earnings. If a company is a serial restructurer or has several pension-accounting factors embedded in earnings, I make the necessary adjustments to the reported earnings number to arrive at the operational cash flow power of the company. I use a multiple that is driven by the growth rate and the return on capital of the company.

When I put a company with a market-like operating cash flow growth rate and a market-like return on capital into my DCF model, the fair value tends to imply that the company should have a forward multiple about the same as that of the market. Note that a consistent relationship between these numbers makes sense because incremental free cash flow drives the DCF value and the two most critical variables that drive incremental free cash flow are the operating cash flow growth rate and return on capital. Stated another way, in practice, the output of the DCF model is predictable and readily approximated if the analyst has the components—an earnings number based on cash flow from operations, the growth rate, and the return on capital.

Applying the Framework. The following examples illustrate how this simple framework can be used. Corvis Corporation, a U.S. communication equipment company, and Transmeta Corporation, a U.S. microprocessor company, are early-stage companies that were projected in 2000 to grow rapidly. During the euphoria of the tech-stock bubble, any tech stock that was beating analysts' revenue estimates was moving higher in price. In this context, scenario analysis was extremely helpful in quantifying the upside potential of a stock based on the price at which it was already trading.

■ *Corvis.* The spreadsheet for Corvis shown in **Table 1** was calculated in October 2000, when the company had a stock price of $67 a share, a multibillion-dollar market cap, and revenues of about $30 million. In the base case, my assumptions were fairly generous. I assumed the company would have 100 percent revenue growth in 2002,[1] 75 percent revenue growth in the following two years, and a 20 percent operating margin by 2004. In the upside case, I projected annual revenue growth of 150 percent in both 2002 and 2003, followed by 100 percent revenue growth. The result was a projected revenue increase from $30 million to $4.3 billion within four years, but the analysis still did not yield a fair value as high as the price at which the stock was trading in the market, as shown in **Table 2**. The scenario analysis produced a fair value of $53 for the upside case, $19 for the base case, and $8 for the downside case. Not surprisingly, it was an easy call not to be interested in Corvis. Its stock price is now less than $1 a share.

■ *Transmeta.* **Table 3** depicts the spreadsheet for Transmeta in February 2001. At that time, the company's stock price was $32 a share. As shown in **Table 4**, the scenario analysis produced a fair value of $49 a share for the upside case, $16 a share for the base case, and $4 a share for the downside case. In the base case, I projected that revenue would grow 60 percent in 2003, followed by revenue growth of 40

---
[1] Years referred to in the analysis of Corvis and Transmeta are their respective fiscal years.

Table 1. Corvis Valuation Framework, October 2000

Case/Category	FY2000	FY2001	FY2002	FY2003	FY2004
Base case					
Revenue (US$ millions)	30	300	600	1,050	1,838
Annual revenue growth	—	—	100%	75%	75%
Operating margin	0.0%	0.0%	10.0	15.0	20.0
Other income as percent of revenue	0.0	0.0	0.0	0.0	0.0
Net margin	0.0	0.0	6.7	10.1	13.4
Net income (US$ millions)	0	0	40	106	246
Shares	328	335	338	342	345
EPS (US$)	—	—	0.12	0.31	0.71
Upside case					
Revenue (US$ millions)	30	350	875	2,188	4,375
Annual revenue growth	—	—	150%	150%	100%
Operating margin	0.0%	0.0%	10.0	15.0	20.0
Other income as percent of revenue	0.0	0.0	0.0	0.0	0.0
Net margin	0.0	0.0	6.7	10.1	13.4
Net income (US$ millions)	—	—	59	220	586
Shares	328	335	335	335	335
EPS (US$)	—	—	0.18	0.66	1.75
Downside case					
Revenue (US$ millions)	30	200	360	540	810
Annual revenue growth	—	—	80%	50%	50%
Operating margin	0.0%	0.0%	10.0	15.0	20.0
Other income as percent of revenue	0.0	0.0	0.0	0.0	0.0
Net margin	0.0	0.0	6.7	10.1	13.4
Net income (US$ millions)	—	—	24	54	109
Shares	328	335	338	342	345
EPS (US$)	—	—	0.07	0.16	0.31

Note: Fiscal year ends in December. Tax rate is 33 percent.

Table 2. Corvis Scenario Analysis: 2004 Forecasts for Base, Upside, and Downside Cases

Parameter	Base	Upside	Downside
EPS	0.71	1.75	0.31
Multiple	45.0	50.0	40.0
Calculated price	$32.1	$87.5	$12.6
Discount period (years)	2.74	2.74	2.74
Required return	20%	20%	20%
Discount factor	0.61	0.61	0.61
Today's value	$19	$53	$8

percent in 2004. The result would be an increase in revenue from $16 million in 2000 to $672 million by 2004. The fair value under the base case was about half the price at which the stock was trading. In the upside case, revenue projections, based on 100 percent and 50 percent revenue growth in 2003 and 2004, respectively, moved from $16 million in 2000 to $1.5 billion in 2004. Based on this scenario, the fair value for the stock was $49 a share. Unlike Corvis, Transmeta at least had an upside fair value greater than the then value of the stock. The next step was to do classic fundamental analysis to assess the likelihood of the various cases coming to pass. In Transmeta's case, some of the key variables were whether its product functionality was superior to Intel's, whether it would be successful in getting hardware manufacturers to adopt its microprocessor, and what Intel's competitive response would be if Transmeta appeared on track to take substantial market share from Intel. The upside case did not come to pass, and the stock price eventually fell below $1 a share.

Current Application. Nokia is not a hyper-growth company, but my simple framework analysis can be helpful because of the high degree of uncertainty about the company's future cash flows.

■ *Nokia*. This analysis is focused on Nokia's U.S. American Depositary Receipt (ADR), which was priced at $17 on 4 November 2002. Thus, spreadsheet

Table 3. Transmeta Valuation Framework, February 2001

Case/Category	FY2000	FY2001	FY2002	FY2003	FY 2004
Base case					
Revenue (US$ thousands)	16,181	134,000	300,000	480,000	672,000
Annual revenue growth	—	—	—	60%	40%
Operating margin	0.0%	0.0%	0.0%	10.0	20.0
Other income as percent of revenue	0.0	0.0	0.0	0.0	0.0
Net margin	0.0	0.0	0.0	6.7	13.4
Net income (US$ thousands)	—	—	—	32,160	90,048
Shares	105,000	129,000	149,000	156,450	164,273
EPS (US$)	—	—	—	$0.21	$0.55
Upside case					
Revenue (US$ thousands)	16,181	200,000	500,000	1,000,000	1,500,000
Annual revenue growth	—	—	—	100%	50%
Operating margin	0.0%	0.0%	0.0%	10.0	25.0
Other income as percent of revenue	0.0	0.0	0.0	0.0	0.0
Net margin	0.0	0.0	0.0	6.7	16.8
Net income (US$ thousands)	—	—	—	67,000	251,250
Shares	105,000	129,000	149,000	156,450	164,272.5
EPS (US$)	—	—	—	0.43	1.53
Downside case					
Revenue (US$ thousands)	16,181	75,000	150,000	225,000	303,750
Annual revenue growth	—	—	—	50%	35%
Operating margin	0.0%	0.0%	0.0%	10.0	15.0
Other income as percent of revenue	0.0	0.0	0.0	0.0	0.0
Net margin	0.0	0.0	0.0	6.7	10.1
Net income (US$ thousands)	—	—	—	15,075	30,526.875
Shares	105,000	129,000	149,000	156,450	164,272.5
EPS (US$)	—	—	—	0.10	0.19

Notes: Tax rate is 29 percent.

Table 4. Transmeta Scenario Analysis: 2004 Forecasts for Base, Upside, and Downside Cases

Parameter	Base	Upside	Downside
EPS	0.55	1.53	0.19
Multiple	45.0	50.0	30.0
Calculated price	$24.7	$76.5	$5.6
Discount period (years)	2.39	2.39	2.39
Required return	20%	20%	20%
Discount factor	0.65	0.65	0.65
Today's value	$16	$49	$4

amounts in **Table 5** are stated in U.S. dollars, but the amounts would not be substantially different if stated in euros. Calendar year (CY) 2001 shows Nokia's actual results. CY 2002, in the base case, shows the consensus sell-side forecasts for revenue and EPS within a penny or two, and CY 2003 incorporates the consensus sell-side forecast for revenue.

In the base case, I assumed 8 percent annual revenue growth and modest operating margin degradation in CY 2004 and CY 2005. The tax rate is a necessary input—in this analysis, I used 29 percent—before net margin, net income, share count, and EPS can be forecast. For CY 2005, forecast EPS is 96 cents. Because I think the company's revenues will grow and the company will earn a return on capital equal to, or perhaps slightly higher than, the market, I used a forward P/E multiple of 17. The result is an estimated market price of $16.30 a share—the price I think the stock will reach by the second half of CY 2004, when the market is discounting forecast earnings for CY 2005. The discount period between the scenario analysis date and the second half of CY 2004 is 1.6 years. I estimate the required return—that is, the return that is necessary for an investor to hold a high-risk stock for the next couple of years—to be 20 percent. Arguably, that number could be lower, and it may be reasonable to use, say, 15 percent. Based on

Table 5. Nokia Valuation Framework, as of 4 November 2002

Case/Category	CY2001	CY2002	CY2003	CY2004	CY2005
Base case					
Revenue (US$ millions)	27,927	29,290	32,738	35,357	38,186
Annual revenue growth	1.0%	4.9%	11.8%	8.0%	8.0%
Operating margin	16.8	17.7	17.2	16.8	16.8
Other income as percent of revenue	0.2	0.2	0.2	0.2	0.2
Net margin	12.1	12.7	12.4	12.1	12.1
Net income (US$ millions)	3,371	3,722	4,044	4,268	4,609
Shares	4,786	4,790	4,797	4,797	4,797
EPS (US$)	0.70	0.78	0.84	0.89	0.96
Upside case					
Revenue (US$ millions)	27,927	29,290	33,684	38,736	44,546
Annual revenue growth	1.0%	4.9%	15%	15%	15%
Operating margin	16.8	17.7	18.0	19.0	20.0
Other income as percent of revenue	0.2	0.2	0.2	0.2	0.2
Net margin	12.1	12.7	12.9	13.6	14.3
Net income (US$ millions)	3,371	3,722	4,353	5,280	6,389
Shares	4,786	4,786	4,642	4,503	4,368
EPS (US$)	0.70	0.78	0.94	1.17	1.46
Downside case					
Revenue (US$ millions)	27,927	29,290	30,755	30,755	30,755
Annual revenue growth	1.0%	4.9%	5%	0%	0%
Operating margin	16.8	17.7	17.2	16.0	15.0
Other income as percent of revenue	0.2	0.2	0.2	0.2	0.2
Net margin	12.1	12.7	12.4	11.5	10.8
Net income (US$ millions)	3,371	3,722	3,799	3,537	3,319
Shares	4,786	4,790	4,797	4,797	4,797
EPS (US$)	0.70	0.78	0.79	0.74	0.69

all of these inputs and assumptions, today's fair value estimate for the base case is $12 a share, as shown in **Table 6**.

In the upside case, I assumed an increase in revenues of 15 percent a year from CY 2003 through CY 2005. In CY 2005, revenues are projected to be $44.5 billion. For these three years, I assumed a slight increase in operating margin and a slight decrease in the number of shares outstanding. I lowered the number of shares outstanding because buying back shares makes sense for a company with a high return on capital and excess cash. It is consistent with the use of a higher multiple. The fair value in the upside case is $22 a share.

In the downside case, I assumed 5 percent annual revenue growth in CY 2003, followed by flat growth for the next two years. I projected a modest decline in operating margin and used a slightly lower multiple (15) than in the base case (17). The fair value in the downside case is $8 a share.

To analyze my outputs, I think in terms of risk and reward rather than a single point estimate. In other words, instead of emphasizing the fair value estimate for the base case, I also analyze the stock's risk–reward potential under both the upside and downside scenarios. This information can be applied in the following way. In early 2002, Nokia's ADR was priced at more than $20, but in July 2002, the price dipped to $10.50. At $10.50, if the analyst focuses on the base-case fair value estimate of $12, Nokia has only modest upside and does not appear to be an interesting investment. But viewed another way, if

Table 6. Nokia Scenario Analysis: 2005 Forecasts for Base, Upside, and Downside Cases

Parameter	Base	Upside	Downside
EPS	0.96	1.46	0.69
Multiple	17.0	20.0	15.0
Calculated price	$16.3	$29.3	$10.4
Discount period (years)	1.65	1.65	1.65
Required return	20%	20%	20%
Discount factor	0.74	0.74	0.74
Today's value	$12	$22	$8

Nokia is at $10.50 with a fair value estimate of $8 in the downside case and $22 in the upside case, Nokia does appear to be attractive.

Of course, scenario analysis assumes that both the upside and downside scenarios have a reasonable chance of occurring. And scenario analysis based on real data is liberating because for a volatile, high-uncertainty company such as Nokia, analysts can have much greater confidence in their estimates of the risk–reward potential for a stock than they can achieve by relying solely on a point estimate. In short, I recommend that analysts shift their focus from a point estimate of the fair value of a stock to a probability distribution of fair *values* for a stock.

For scenario analysis to be successful, the assumptions for the upside and downside cases must be stable and should not be changed each time the company reports. I cannot emphasize this point enough; the upside and downside cases must have a solid, data-driven foundation that is not influenced by short-term business results. My view of Nokia's upside being $44 billion in revenues is driven by a forecast of estimated market revenues for the total handset industry, Nokia's market share, wireless infrastructure revenues, and market size. The same holds true for the downside case; the assumptions are relatively objective and are based on the overall industry's market characteristics. The base case, however, should be updated with new information about Nokia. For example, if Nokia was to report higher-than-anticipated operating margins in the last quarter, the base case should be adjusted but the upside and downside cases usually should be unaffected.

Scenario analysis is an important contribution to valuation because stock prices tend to react to near-term events. With the recent proliferation of long–short hedge funds, more market participants have become more short-term oriented and aggressively trade on actual or anticipated datapoints. With a longer-term view and a risk–reward perspective, analysts can take advantage of the near-term moves in the stock price to buy (sell) when they think the risk–reward potential is attractive (unattractive) within the context of solid scenario analysis.

Conclusion

Analysts need to recognize the difficulties and risks involved in using traditional present value methodologies, such as a DCF model, to value high-growth, nontraditional companies. Although such companies are often thought of as being almost exclusively high tech, many other sectors have high uncertainty. An adjustment to the standard valuation methodology for hypergrowth/high-uncertainty companies includes conceptually distinguishing between the hypergrowth period and the subsequent period of more normal growth. Scenario analysis is also a powerful adjustment to the traditional DCF approach.

The three-case scenario analysis approach provides a particularly useful alternative to a single-point valuation that expresses little about the upside potential or downside risk involved in holding a particular stock. Because the scenario analysis approach with full DCF models for each scenario can be time-consuming, I developed a simple valuation framework that uses a forecast forward P/E at the end of the company's hypergrowth period and the estimated appreciation in stock price during the hypergrowth phase. This framework is flexible enough to use on a daily basis and incorporates the same basic inputs of the DCF model. I have found it to be useful and effective in practice.

Question and Answer Session

Barney H. Wilson

Question: Will the real options method ever become a viable valuation tool?

Wilson: A simple approach can be powerful but too basic; likewise, a complex approach that can incorporate many different variables can be too sophisticated. On the spectrum of complexity, my scenario analysis is extremely simple. In my view, the real options method is too complex to use on a daily basis to value individual stocks. Nonetheless, many of the concepts of the real options method are embedded in scenario analysis. The base case and downside case, for instance, are the less-risky scenarios for a company's cash flows, and the upside case, which attempts to quantify the positive options, or how high the cash flows and stock price can go, represents the riskier scenario.

Question: How do you determine probabilities, given that the critical valuation variables are subjectively determined?

Wilson: The opportunity to make money in individual stocks lies in being right more often than you are wrong, and the entire decision-making process is highly subjective. An analyst's skill is determined by his or her understanding of the industry structure and ability to make a reasonable forecast. An analyst adds value by making a bold call on partial information; once complete information becomes available, it has already been factored into the stock price. I recommend acknowledging the high degree of subjectivity that is involved in the process and getting as much data as possible to support your call.

Question: Why do you choose 20 percent as the required return discounting factor?

Wilson: Twenty percent is somewhat arbitrary, but it seems an appropriate return to me (as an investor) to justify holding a risky stock. The better number may be 15 percent, but I do not think it is as low as 10 percent. A 10 percent return would not justify holding a risky stock.

Question: How can the expected value from traditional DCF analysis not be meaningful?

Wilson: Determining expected value is a logical number-crunching exercise, but it will not help an analyst pick money-making stocks. If the exercise is simply to find the average of the expected value of disparate outcomes, the analyst's attention is deflected away from where he or she can really add insight and value. As I said, the expected value is often the least-likely outcome because it is merely the average value of the possible outcomes. Consider the Transmeta example. The stock price was $32, and it was either going to $4 or $50. The contribution of an analyst rests in figuring out which is more likely, $4 or $50. There is not much to be gained in focusing on the average of the two numbers.

Question: Does your approach work with private equity valuation?

Wilson: Absolutely. Scenario analysis is used by private equity investors who invest in early-stage technology companies. Venture capitalists want to invest in companies that will eventually acquire large market share. Thus, the upside for a company and the probability of meeting that upside, not the average of all possible outcomes, are the important issues to the venture capitalist.

Question: How do you select the number of years to forecast company data? Does it vary from company to company?

Wilson: The number is driven by the investment horizon. My primary investment horizon is one year, but sometimes, it is 18 months or two years. In the scenario analysis for a stock I want to buy today, I ask where the stock price is likely to be a year or two from now, and that's what drives my choice of investment horizon. I would be tempted, however, to increase the number of years in the horizon for a company that, in my view, might take longer to achieve a stable business model.

Question: Are technology companies still overvalued?

Wilson: I tend to avoid saying in public forums whether I believe a particular group of stocks is overvalued or undervalued. That said, I think some tech companies are overvalued at today's prices. Most technology companies are forecasting 20–30 percent revenue growth for the next couple of years, but such rapid growth is unlikely for the tech sector as a whole. Keep in mind that the market is extremely volatile, so a sector that is overvalued at a certain date may not be overvalued a month later. For example, in September and early October 2002, the Philadelphia Stock Exchange Semiconductor Index, or the SOX (a price-weighted index composed of 17 U.S. companies primarily involved in the design, distribution, manufacture, and sale of semiconductors), was 50 percent lower than in early November 2002. Many semiconductor stocks were attractive on a risk–reward basis at the time but are not now.